"I've long admired Pam Hendrickson's unquestionably unique talent for organizing content and packaging products in a way that's incredibly compelling—and effective for influencing her audience. She's worked with some of the best and brightest minds of today, many of whom I count as close friends, and I've seen first-hand the tremendous impact she's had on their businesses. In the *Art of Impact*, she'll show you how to share the message you were born to deliver so it gets heard—and acted on."

JOHN ASSARAF, NY Times Bestselling Author, Founder and CEO of PraxisNow.com

"What if you could learn the secret of impacting millions of lives in a single short book? If you're intrigued by this idea, then you're in the right place at the right time.

Turning ideas into useful content and package content into products is an extremely rare skill that requires systems, patience and practice. Pam Hendrickson has distilled over 25 years of knowledge - her life's work into an extremely readable guide. You should know Pam inherited a teacher's DNA from her mom who developed training tools that have transformed the lives of millions of young musicians, worldwide.

Pam's work has been delivered to millions of clients throughout her career - and when you implement a few of the ideas in this book, you could do the same."

MIKE KOENIGS, Serial Entreprenuer and 10-Time #1 Bestselling Author

"Since our Anthony Robbins days, I have always been impressed with Pam Henrickson's ability to transform a tremendous amount of information into a comprehensive system that anyone can immediately implement to get results. When it comes to content, she is one of my go-to experts."

AMY PORTERFIELD, Social Media Strategy Consultant, Co-Author of *Facebook All-in-One For Dummies*

"My whole life has been about two things: having an IMPACT and being the BEST. When I left the NFL, I had no idea what I was going to do. Little did I know that "distributing content" would be my next career and that it would lead to speaking, writing, performing, as well as coaching and training others for peak performance. If I had this guide back then, it would have saved me thousands of hours of time, energy and mistakes. No matter what format your content is, Pam gives you the keys to the kingdom to create a content map that will help you transform audiences and build massive momentum in your business. When it comes to my business and life, I only work with the best and Pam is the absolute BEST in this area!"

BO EASON, Former NFL Standout, Acclaimed Broadway Playwright and Performer, and International Story/Peak Performance Coach

"For more than 25 years I have had the amazing privilege of calling Pam Hendrickson my friend, my mentor and my teacher. There is a reason why the best of the best and the brightest of the brightest come to Pam for her guidance and creative input. I am thrilled that she is bringing her brilliance to the world now. There's no one better to help you take your ideas and turn them into an effective message that will move your audience to action."

JOSEPH MCCLENDON III, Peak Performance Specialist, Corporate Trainer & Best-Selling Author

"Pam Hendrickson is the "Top Gun" of content marketing. There's no one better. No one. And this book is an easy-to-read, easy-to-execute treatise on how to (relatively) effortlessly attract high quality clients simply by using what you already know.

Having consulted over 300 companies, I can tell you from first-hand experience that most "content marketing plans" are the kind of dart-board guesswork you would expect from the village idiot. At best, they don't work (like your nephew Ronnie). And at worse, they are wildly embarrassing (like your drunk Uncle Tony).

Seriously, read this book. Do what Pam recommends. For in doing so, not only will you create a raving new band of fans...but you'll also find they're relatively easy to turn into customers (now that they believe you, know you, and trust you)."

ED RUSH, 4-Time #1 Selling Author, 7-Figure Consultant, and Former Fighter Pilot

"This book is a must-read for any speaker or author. I've been working with speakers and authors for over a decade and I'm going to make it a requirement from this point forward that they read this book so they can avoid any costly content marketing mistakes. This book is a gold mine, jammed-packed with relevant information to make sure your content converts!"

JESSIE SCHWARTZBURG, Event Producer and Author/Speaker Consultant

"When you discover that you have a message to share with the world, you need to figure out the best way to bring your idea to fruition. Pam Hendrickson's book, The Art Of Impact, provides the pathway to create and curate your message so that you can attract your perfect audience, and create a business you love.

By her example, Pam will motivate you to move forward with motivation and courage. She'll teach you how to create something extraordinary that is uniquely you. Pam is my go-to content and marketing guru. She's the expert I listen to, and I do what she says. Read her book, be inspired, and watch your dream unfold."

SUSAN BURLINGAME, Author, *Kick-Ass Corporate Wife*

The
Art of

IMPACT

How to Use Content Marketing the Right Way to Build Your Brand, Grow Your Business and Make a Difference

PAM HENDRICKSON

#1 best-selling author, entrepreneur and content strategist

For More Resources:
www.PamHendrickson.com/Impact

ISBN: 978-0-692-62165-3

Published by:
Content Solutions Group, Inc.
3830 Valley Centre Drive, #705-314
San Diego, CA 92130

866-654-6534 or 858-720-8720

www.PamHendrickson.com

Disclaimer: No portion of this material is intended to offer legal, medical, personal or financial advice. We've taken every effort to ensure we accurately represent these strategies and their potential to help you grow your business. However, we do not purport this as a "get rich scheme" and there is no guarantee that you will earn any money using the content, strategies or techniques displayed here. Nothing in this presentation is a promise or guarantee of earnings. The content, case studies and examples shared in this book do not in any way represent the "average" or "typical" member experience. In fact, as with any product or service, we know that some members purchase our systems and never use them, and therefore get no results from their membership whatsoever. Therefore, the member case studies we are sharing can neither represent nor guarantee the current or future experience of other past, current or future members. Rather, these member case studies represent what is possible with our system. Each of these unique case studies, and any and all results reported in these case studies by individual members, are the culmination of numerous variable, many of which we cannot control, including pricing, target market conditions, product/service quality, offer, customer service, personal initiative, and countless other tangible and intangible factors. Your level of success in attaining similar results is dependent upon a number of factors including your skill, knowledge, ability, connections, dedication, business savvy, business focus, business goals, and financial situation. Because these factors differ according to individuals, we cannot guarantee your success, income level, or ability to earn revenue. You alone are responsible for your actions and results in life and business, and by your use of these materials, you agree not to attempt to hold us liable for any of your decisions, actions or results, at any time, under any circumstance. The information contained herein cannot replace or substitute for the services of trained professionals in any field, including, but not limited to, financial or legal matters. Under no circumstances, including but not limited to negligence, will Pam Hendrickson, Content Solutions Group, Inc. or any of its representatives or contractors be liable for any special or consequential damages that result from the use of, or the inability to use, the materials, information, or success strategies communicated through these materials, or any services following these materials, even if advised of the possibility of such damages.

DEDICATION

To my mom.

"What cannot be achieved in one lifetime will happen when one lifetime is joined to another."
—Harold Kushner

ACKNOWLEDGMENTS

To my saint of a husband, Chris, and my two boys, Jon and Ben. You are my everything, and I love you with all my heart.

To the talented and wonderful Jill Blessing, who so elegantly captured the essence of my message on paper.

To Lisa Rothstein, for sharing your art and humor with us throughout this book.

To my small and mighty team: Gina Onativia, Alex Espinosa, Megan O'Leary and Erin Marshall. Chris and I are very, very grateful for who you are and all you do.

To our amazing clients and colleagues. It is an honor to be on this entrepreneurial path with you.

To our partners, JVs, colleagues and friends. Thanks for your partnership, support, wisdom and coaching when I've needed it!

ILLUSTRATIONS

 Lisa Rothstein is the award-winning Madison Avenue ad agency copywriter and creative director best known for creating the famous "Wait'll We Get Our Hanes on You" campaign that changed America's underwear. In her own consulting business, she uses cartooning, insightful copy and cutting-edge strategy to help corporations and entrepreneurs see their ideal clients, products, brand mission and message in a new and unforgettable way. She is a graduate of Brown University with a degree in Semiotics. (Ask Pam if you don't know what that is!) www.LisaRothstein.com

Contents

INTRODUCTION

"Inside every block of marble dwells a beautiful statue."
—*Michelangelo*

You have a gift.

There is something you have to share with the world. And *only* you can deliver it.

I know this because I learned it about myself… but it took me a while to get there.

From the time I was a little girl, it was clear that I should follow "the plan." Now, this plan was never spoken about. It was never written down. It was simply clear that if I wanted to have a successful life, I should follow it. And so I did.

I did well in school. I sang in the church choir. I was in the thespian society and had the lead in almost every school play. I played a piano concerto with the youth orchestra. I was president of the honor society. I graduated valedictorian of my high school. I attended an Ivy League School, and graduated Magna Cum Laude from Brown University. I dated all the "right" guys, i.e., the future doctors and lawyers of my generation.

And when I graduated from college, I was rewarded with a bright, new, shiny black Volkswagon Jetta.

It seemed like I was on track with American dream, right? But deep down, I felt unsettled. It just took a near-death experience for me to admit it to myself.

A few months later, after graduation, I was driving my VW Jetta from Providence, Rhode Island, back to my parents' house in western New York state, rocking out to Joni Mitchell, and thinking about my life so far. And, as I crossed over the border into the mountains of New York, it started to snow...

And the roads started to get bad. But I was familiar with driving in winter conditions and was feeling alert, but pretty in control.

Until I hit a patch of ice... on a bridge. And the car began to swerve all over the road.

But I thought to myself, "I got this. I know what to do. I was taught how to follow the rules to handle this type of situation. I have a plan— just don't break and turn into the skid."

So, that is exactly what I did. But it didn't work.

The car spun around and came to sudden and loud stop, jolting me with the impact. Everything went still for a single second. Slowly, I opened my eyes, and all I could see in front of me was a raging, cold, scary river looking back up at me. My car had hit the guardrail and was now hanging precariously over the water, much too close to it for my comfort. In this moment of chaos and total confusion, all I could think was, "This is *not* the plan."

I honestly can't remember how I got out of my car that day. My adrenaline kicked in, and somehow I climbed out without tipping the car over the railing—thankfully. I then began to do what I suspect most anyone would do in my situation—I started flailing my arms around, like a crazy person, in an effort to flag a good Samaritan down from the side of the road.

And as I was standing there on the side of the road, parts of my life started to flash by. I began thinking about the future lawyer I was dating and how he barely had any time for me. I wondered what it would be like when he was actually working full-time for a law firm.

I thought about my then current job working in a sleep research laboratory, where I had literally been staying up all night to watch people sleep.

And as I think about all of this, I recognize something that perhaps I had hadn't had the courage to see before. I realized that the "plan" I had been playing out was not the plan that was in my heart. It was not the plan that was going to make me truly happy in life. It was not really *my* plan. This was a turning point.

That night, from a drafty hotel room somewhere in the middle of New York state, after being rescued by two friendly passersby, I wrote for several hours in my journal. And the gist of my take-away was this: *What do you do when the life you've been living up to now isn't getting you what you really want?*

Whoa. Big question.

I had grown up around the world of personal development. On family road-trips, my parents would listen to speakers like Earl Nightengale. In fact, as a 9-year-old, I was already very familiar with Nightengale's "strangest secret," i.e., the idea that you become what you think about.

So coming to this conclusion left me in unfamiliar territory. Up until that point, I had always known what to go for next and how to feel accomplished. And when I finally arrived home to tell my parents that I didn't want to be doing what I was doing anymore, and that I didn't know *what* I wanted to do instead, they were kind and supportive, but worried as well.

Their solution? To promptly send me to California to attend a Tony Robbins seminar they hoped would "fix me."

Now remember, I had been forced to listen to personal development tapes during family vacations for my entire life, and so this was the *last* thing I really wanted to do. *But*, I reasoned— it *was* a free trip to beautiful California… and I didn't have anything better to do. And so off to sunny San Diego I went.

The trip ended up being more than worth it. While there, I learned two key things that have actually impacted everything I have done since:

First, *every person has the personal responsibility to decide what he or she will think, feel, do. No one can do this for you.*

And second, *if you know specifically what you want, the pathway to achieve it is to access a proven system that will show you step-by-step how to get there and then to unblock anything that might be in the way of you achieving your goal.*

In fact, these two pivotal lessons are ultimately what this book is about—to share the tools I've learned over the years to help you own, master and conquer your content marketing. However, my driving force and what I really want to impart to you within the pages of this book is more than that.

Because my deeper life epiphany came a few decades later…

After the event in California, I ended up working for Tony Robbins' core company—first as a switchboard operator (at which I failed miserably), then as a transcriptionist, and eventually as the Vice President of Content and Product Development. It was an amazing career for which I'm really proud and grateful.

And when I left 18 years later, it wasn't because the job wasn't great, and it wasn't because I was tired all over again of personal development. It was because I got to this point where I realized that no matter what—I was ultimately *never going to achieve the income and impact I was looking for until I stopped trading my time for money.*

Time, I started to realize, is irreplaceable and finite. Money, on the other hand, is more versatile. It can be made and replaced in other ways… ways that might give me more time to be with the people I love…and ways that would have more upside where I was in control.

Unbeknownst to me at the time, this lesson was extraordinarily timely. The rich value of time spent with loved ones became suddenly acute that year… when I lost someone very special.

Behind everything that I had done in my life up to this point, there had been one single person who made the most impact on my core and who I was as a person. One single person who had simultaneously been my friend, cheerleader, sage, mentor, glue and rock.

That person was my mother.

She was a piano teacher who traveled the world lecturing parents and teachers about how to empower children to learn. She was a resilient champion and believer in helping others express their unique gifts. She was a leader and a confidant to more people than I even know. In fact, what the people she taught learned about music was inevitably secondary to the life lessons my mother shared and the confidence she built in them.

She believed that the job of an educator was to chip away at whatever was getting in the way of each person's ability to express and share his or her authentic and brilliant value (which was, in retrospect, why she had forced me to listen to so many of those annoying personal development tapes growing up). For her entire life, my mother was an impressive role model, working to help others see just how great they could be.

And so… the day I found out my mom was going to die was, without a doubt, the worst day of my life.

I was back East in one of those crazy little doctors' offices that are about as big as a postage stamp, sitting in there with my mom, as we waited for the doctor to come in. There was a hustle of activity outside the room, but inside as we waited, it was still—just my mom and me.

We are both talkers, and we always have something to converse and chat about. Yet, in that moment, only silence hovered between us. What do you say when you are waiting for the most important news of your entire life together? We sat there together in silence for what seemed like forever, until finally the doctor appeared.

The news was simple. He didn't even walk all the way into the office to share it. He just kind of stood at the door, looked at my mom, and said, "Carole, it's not good news. The tests came back, and the fluid around your lungs is full of cancer."

My mom softly closed her eyes, looked up and said, "How long?"

The doctor replied, "I don't know. I'm going to refer you to an oncologist, but I'm hoping for six or 12 months."

My mom stated simply, "Okay." And he left.

Three days later, I was sitting in her hospital room. She had just gotten out of the ICU and was meeting her oncologist for the first time. He had all of her charts and information, but hadn't met with her personally yet to share his diagnosis.

As he entered the room, he saw that she was sleeping. So he directed his attention to my brother and me. Shaking his head, he said to us, "I'd be surprised if she makes it through the night, and I want you to be prepared."

There were no words. My brother and I just sat there in silence for a while, until my brother finally decided to go get something to eat.

I found myself alone with my mother in her semi-conscious state, sharing what could potentially be our last moments together. And I was completely lost and confused. So I did the only think I could think to do—I crawled into bed with her.

As a curled up next to her, she stirred, and I said to her, "Mom, is this okay?"

And she said quietly, "I love it."

Then... I whispered in her ear everything that was in my heart.

I told her that I knew was she was scared, and that I am too. But more than the pain, I am grateful. I told her that I wound not change one day or do one thing different for the opportunity for her to be my mom. I reminded her that she and I had a special bond and a connection that goes well beyond the physical and into the spiritual. And I reminded her that the spiritual connection would never go away.

I told her I'm so grateful she's been here for me for every major life event you can imagine—growing up, concerts, plays, school graduation, the tough times, high school, college, my wedding, the birth of my boys, my babies. How lucky am I for that? I told her that I'll miss her so much, but that I promise to keep the memories alive for me, for my two boys, Jon and Ben, and for my family.

I told her I'd do things like take my boys to the Jersey shore, like she used to do for us every summer. I told her that I'd do things for my nieces, Margaret and Laura, and that I will keep so many of the traditions living for us.

"Most of all," I told her, "Mom, I just want you to know that the core of who I am comes from you. It's inseparable. It's how I live my life. It's the wisdom I use to raise my boys. It's how I'll know what to do when times get tough."

These moments with my mom made me realize in a deep, grave, important way—*life is fleeting*. And that is exactly what makes it so precious.

Before my mom was diagnosed, I always thought that the whole secret to success and happiness was achieving. I believed that it was the answer not only to a successful life, but that it would make everyone around me happy.

To say I've changed my thinking would be an understatement.

In essence, I realized that working hard was great, but that coming home every night at 8 p.m., rushing in the door barely with enough time to kiss my kids goodnight was going to leave me missing out on a huge part of what's most important.

And that's changed everything.

In the end, my mom lived six weeks past the time that the doctor came into the hospital room, shook his head, and said she wasn't going to live through the night. It was long enough for her to see her grandchildren again. It was long enough for her to go home. It was long enough for us to spend time with her and for her to pass on her own terms, which is amazing.

Always pushing the envelope, my mom rarely, if ever, underestimated anyone or anything. Yet in the days before she passed away, she made only one short-sighted prediction. She said to me, "Honey, you are not going to be able to speak at my service, and it's okay. There are just going to be a few people there from the church. Just go and just read a few of these notes and letter here, and it'll be fine. It's okay."

While touching and well-intentioned, she couldn't have been more wrong. When I arrived at the church for her services, there was standing room only. Over 600 people from all over the world filled the room. In fact, the room was so packed, we had to pipe in a video feed to the Fellowship Hall because everyone wouldn't fit into the main sanctuary. And I was, in fact, too inspired by her impact not to speak. Even in death, her radiance overshadowed my grief.

Looking around at all of these people, I noticed that these people were not just acquaintances who my mom may have run into at the grocery store or post office in a collection of fleeting moments; every person in the room had an incredibly sincere and powerful connection with her. These were people whose lives she had deeply affected. They were people she had inspired—by always seeing more in them then they saw in themselves. She had been with them to celebrate their victories, and she had been there to help them get through their deepest challenges, darkest times, and biggest defeats.

In that moment, I realized that my mom had never been afraid of dying. She was afraid of any of us *not really living*.

I lost my mom that day, but it was also the day that I found my voice. It was the day that I stepped into my own gifts and declared that my courage would win over my fear, and that somehow, in some way, I'd find a way to continue her legacy of deeply inspiring and empowering others to really, truly, fully *live*.

So with my entire heart, I dedicate this book to two things—first, to my beautiful mother, Carole Bigler.

And second, to you—the person holding this book in your hands. May you live the life that no one else can live and focus on achieving what *you* really want. May you put yourself at the driver's seat and take total personal responsibility for what you think, feel and do. May you look for life's short-cuts by finding masters you can emulate to accomplish your dreams. May you not get trapped in the roller-coaster illusion of trading time for money.

And most importantly, may you *really live*. May you understand the impact that you uniquely have. May you use your precious time to focus on what's most important. May you boldly, brightly, brilliantly share *your* gifts with the world. And may you inspire others to do the same.

Pam Hendrickson
February 2016

"

You come into this world with nothing.
You leave this world with nothing.
All you have is what you give while you're here.

—Dr. Wayne W. Dyer

Pam Hendrickson

PART ONE

THE 5 MASTER STEPS OF CONTENT THAT CONVERTS

NOTE: The lessons in this section are based on the five master steps of content that connects and converts. Use these content strategies to attract your ideal audience, build relationships and close more sales.

11

THE 5 MASTER STEPS

Step 1:   Create Content That's Relevant

Step 2:   Attract—and Keep—Your Audience's Attention

Step 3:   Develop Your Signature Talk

Step 4:   Produce Great Content With Speed

Step 5:   Maximize Your Content Distribution

CHAPTER ONE
THE SQUEAKY WHEEL NO LONGER GETS THE GREASE

"The great aim of education is not knowledge, but action."
—*Herbert Spencer*

In the last 3 minutes…

- $7,206,000 has been spent on online training, products, apps and downloads worldwide.

- 144,000 apps were downloaded from Apple's App Store.

- $46,053 was spent on apps, and that was just on Apple.

- $13,698 was spent on personal coaching.

- $62,758 was spent on personal development.

- Amazon earned over $250,000.

- YouTube users uploaded 216,000 hours of video.

- 7-11 sold 558 Slurpees.

That last one is just for fun. (And frankly, I'm not even sure how they sold a single cup, that stuff is so bad for you!) But here's my point. How much of this money went into *your* bank account?

Because if your content message isn't leading to the money, it means it's not having the impact you're likely seeking.

Here's some insight as to where the problem may lie:

The average person currently consumes and shares a staggering amount of information. With every passing minute...

- Email users send an average 204,000,000 messages.

- Facebook users share 2,460,000 pieces of content.

- Twitter users tweet 277,000 times.

- Pinterest users pin 3,472 images.

- YouTube users upload 72 hours of new video.

- Google receives over 4,000,000 search queries.

In addition, we now have access to more people on the planet than ever before. The global Internet population now totals a staggering 2.4 billion people. And that's just an estimate.

People are consuming (and responding) to content absolutely *everywhere*...

75 percent of Americans even admit to bringing their phone into the bathroom, 70 percent of phone searches lead to online action within an hour, and statistics show that more people now own smartphones than toothbrushes (almost 2 billion people).

And this is where the disconnect occurs for many businesses. There is so much opportunity available today to get your message in front of anyone, anywhere in the world, almost instantly, with the click of a button.

The challenge is, none of this matters much if you don't have an audience (or the right audience) in the first place, or if you don't have a strategy to *move* your audience to action.

That's where content marketing comes in.

In the official words of the Content Marketing Institute, content marketing is, "the marketing and business process for creating and distributing relevant and valuable content to attract, acquire, and engage a clearly defined and understood target audience."

In short, content marketing is subtle. It's not the interruption-based, in-your-face, marketing that defined the beginning of the traditional advertising era many years ago. It's about building a connection and *earning* the trust and attention of your audience by providing real value in format they can easily respond and relate to. When done correctly, content marketing has the potential to help a business build a base of loyal customers, establish brand recognition and trust, and drive ongoing sales.

However, content marketing is both overused and underused as a marketing tool in today's world. Whereas there is a lot of information out there, there is little that is created with the precision and sincerity necessary to effectively build a positive relationship with readers.

Let me give you a sense of just how much information is currently being generated in the world. We now create as much information every two days as we have from the dawn of civilization up to 2003. Let me repeat that—in just *two days*, we put as much data out there as we did from *the dawn* of civilization to 2003. That's an insane of information. And as a result, as consumers, we are overwhelmed.

55 percent of people who click on a link to an article spend less than 15 seconds reading it.

We will devote only 60 to 120 seconds to a video before turning it off.

When browsing the web, the average person has an attention span of about 8 seconds—that's one second less than the attention span of a goldfish!

TRUE TO FORM, GOLDIE DEMONSTRATES
HIS SUPERIOR ATTENTION SPAN...

What's more? This number is decreasing. Back in 2000, our attention span was 50 percent greater—we used to spend up to 12 minutes perusing a site before moving on.

> *We are drowning in information, while starving for wisdom. The world henceforth will be run by synthesizers, people able to put together the right information at the right time, think critically about it, and make important choices wisely.*
>
> —*E.O. Wilson*

We are overwhelmed by the quantity of sources constantly vying for our attention. And as a result, being loud is not enough anymore. The old adage that the squeakiest wheel will get the grease is no longer true, at least not in the realm of information sharing.

The average person receives 5,000 marketing messages per day. 78 percent of people are on the "Do Not Call" list. 94 percent of TV viewers leave the room or change the channel during advertisements, 44 percent of people never open anything that even remotely resembles direct mail, and 90 percent of emails received are deleted before they are read. In all, 60-70 percent of traditional marketing content is completely ignored.

In today's world, it's not just about getting your information out there. That's not enough. In order to capture someone's attention, you have to share information in a *meaningful* way.

People are smarter now. We have to be. We don't just want to know about data. We want to know what data means *to us*. We are forced to tune out the bland, the overdone, and the constant noise around us, and yet we are hungry, *starving* for something real.

So, what do we really want? What will stop us in our tracks and give you our undivided attention?

People want *excellence*. We want to learn how to excel and advance our lives in a meaningful way. We want to excel and grow in a way that matters *to us*. We want to solve our biggest, most urgent problems and use that as a catalyst to achieve the next level in our lives. We want real data, from a real human, that speaks to a very real and immediate need in our lives.

As a marketer, if you can meet this need, if you can give us real tools for ongoing excellence in our lives, you will acquire a base of loyal customers who will happily indulge in the content you offer. You will have so many fans, your challenge will be coming up with ways to serve us all at the same time.

Indeed, the secret to providing real and relevant content that *sells* is to carve out a clear and obtainable path to excellence.

But... you may be thinking, excellence is different to everyone, isn't it? Some people want to improve their finances in order to retire early. Others are battling health concerns and are looking for new ways to improve their wellbeing. Still others just want a great and healthy relationship.

It's true—the pursuit of excellence is absolutely different (and always evolving) for everyone. The same is true for the problems and obstacles that are in our way. And because the potential needs are so vast, and the potential reach is now so far, the key lies in providing ultra-niche solutions. Specificity is paramount to content success.

Which is precisely where you come in and why *your unique message* is so important. Since no one else has the specific set of life lessons and experiences as you, no one can offer the same level of mastery in your very distinct area of expertise as *you*.

Ultimately, this must be the goal of your content—to speak directly to a superbly targeted audience in order to solve a very specific problem, using an original and specially designed formula that delivers the right kind of excellence to the right person. This is what will make your content real and relevant. It is will make it meaningful, and it is will make your audience care about what you have to say.

Regardless of the medium you choose—social media, webcasting, webinars, web pages, articles, eBooks, live events, etcetera, etcetera—these are all simply known ways to communicate with your audience. But at the end of the day, these are just vehicles.

To make your content effective, you need to take step back and look at your entire system. Because unless the *message* that's behind your business model is compelling and clear, unless it's targeted toward a very special and unique audience, and unless that message is providing value that helps them achieve excellence in their endeavors, it will not have the impact you are looking for.

Do you know the core message that is currently driving your business? Is it working?

CHAPTER ONE: THE BIG TAKE-AWAY

Content marketing is about connecting your knowledge to the value it will bring a very targeted audience by helping them achieve excellence through a systematic, easy-to-follow series of clear steps.

The key is your core message: Does it solve a burning problem your audience has? Does it contain the emotion that will get you audience to care and act upon.

CHAPTER 1: RESOURCES

To improve upon or build your content marketing techniques, consider the following:

People consume and share content that...

1   Evokes a positive emotion (awe, joy, surprise are the top 3 favorites). People want to feel good, and they want the people they care about to feel good too. Entertaining ideas, engaging stories, funny anecdotes or metaphors, content that evokes laughter and fun, simple *human* concepts are the most shared items online.

2   Is original. There is a lot of repetition found online, and people get tired of sifting through the clutter. It's rare and refreshing to find something new, different and totally original. Google gives original, new works better rankings, as well, making them easier to find.

3   Is personalized to their needs and interests. People are attracted to what is meaningful to *them*. This is why 79 percent of web users scan versus read. They are constantly asking themselves: What here is relevant *to me*? Why do I care? What is most important for me to know? Is any of this worth my time?

4   Communicates an idea creatively and succinctly, such as an infographic. Visual elements can help a lot in making a complex subject easy to understand quickly, which is why people are drawn to both consume and share them.

5   Is practical and relevant. People want to read about current events and or meaningful new data that solves an immediate and specific need.

People will pay for...

1   Insight or tips about a relevant topic that they cannot get anywhere else.

2   Information or videos that are exclusive, or behind the scenes. To meet this demand, many publications and music sites offer a premium version.

3   On-demand access to content they can come back to when they want, such as digital music, software, apps, games, videos, photos, ebooks, podcasts, etcetera.

4   An "expert" education, such as an nontraditional online MBA offered by a trusted thought leader.

5   A sense of community with groups they care about, i.e., membership sites.

6   Higher quality reporting or information. This is especially true for higher-income brackets. In fact, more than 300 newspapers now charge some kind of fee for digital content.

7   Services that filter and personalize information. Many people don't have the time to gather quality information on their own. Consistent reliability and accuracy make this type of service extremely valuable to students, educators and those in research fields.

8   Convenience. People enjoy the ability to view information offline and/or to access it in multiple places. Spotify is a good example of this—their premier service enables people to take their playlists with them and to play music "offline."

9   Clean and simple viewing without distractions. We are so tired of being bombarded with advertisements, we will pay to avoid them.

❝

*The great aim of education is not knowledge,
but action.*

—Herbert Spencer

CHAPTER TWO
THE "FLOP" AT L'ENFANT STATION

"It's not what you look at that matters, it's what you see."
—Henry David Thoreau

I have some good news for you.

To make your content marketing stand out and gain the traction you desire, odds are you need to work at least a little *less*.

In fact, the biggest mistake most business owners make in terms of content marketing is that they put too much out there of the wrong thing.

It's not that they're not creating *enough* content. It's not that they need to spend more money on a fancy campaign. It's not that they need a professionally filmed series of videos to garner sales. It simply this—they are distributing...

the **wrong content**,
to the **wrong people**,
at the **wrong time**.

By trying to hit a moving and ambiguous target, most content marketers are stuck spinning their wheels while feeling overwhelmed and exhausted. Even worse, they are unsure if all of their efforts are even *really* working because they don't have a solid way to measure the results.

But they don't know what to do instead either, and so they just keep on putting out more… and more… and more. They work on making their e-books more thoughtful, their videos more professional, their social media more clever, and their case studies more engaging. They spend money on elaborate designs and beat themselves up for letting their blog slip for a week or two. They are consumed and even a little obsessed with this ongoing struggle to maintain a standard of constantly streaming content.

I've been there. It's frustrating. And daunting. And never-ending…

And there is a way out.

If I had to sum up the single most important thing you should remember about content marketing in a single word, it would be this—context.

In terms of making your content something that people notice, engage with, and respond to, more is not a productive (or sustainable) outcome, but *context* is. In fact, as it relates to the effectiveness of your content marketing results, context is *everything*. For all of the work you might put into a descriptive e-book, dynamic video series, or beautifully designed info-graphic, it is actually all for naught without context.

Let me give you an example of what I mean.

There is a famous story written by Gene Weingarten of *The Washington Post* entitled, *Pearls Before Breakfast*. (If you haven't already read it, Google it. It's worth the read.)

Here is the gist of the story.

Weingarten approached world-renowned violinist, Joshua Bell, and asked him if he would consider being part of a social experiment—Bell was to put on street clothes and perform at rush hour in Washington D.C.'s L'Enfant Metro Station, totally incognito. The outcome was to see if people would be able to recognize his talent in this unusual context.

Keep in mind—Bell is an internationally acclaimed virtuoso violinist. Just three days before the experiment, he filled the house at Boston Symphony Hall, where merely good seats sold for $100 and the entire concert brought in $115,000. In short, under normal circumstances, Bell is paid at a premium for his extolled talents, usually around $1,000 per minute.

In addition, prior to the experiment, editors at *The Post Magazine* were worried about how they would handle crowd control if things were to get out of hand. They anticipated that a large crowd might gather in the subway as people began to recognize Bell and word started to spread about what was happening. Masses of people, they presumed, would want to take advantage of the opportunity to hear such an extraordinary musician perform for free.

Here is what actually happened.

Bell began playing in the subway station on his 1713 Stradivarius violin, which, by the way, is worth $3.5 million. He started with Bach's Chaccone, which is universally accepted among master violists as one of the most difficult pieces to master. In total, Bell played for about 45 minutes straight, all the while exhibiting the same level of expertise, dedication and passion that he would have embodied at an elite event for a crowded concert hall.

But in spite of all of that energy, enthusiasm and raw art, not only did few people stop to enjoy Bell's performance, he was largely... *ignored* completely by the busy commuters who hurried past.

In Weingarten's article, he writes:

"...seven people stopped what they were doing to hang around and take in the performance, at least for a minute. 27 gave money, most of them on the run — for a total of $32 and change. That leaves 1,070 people who hurried by, oblivious, many only three feet away, few even turning to look."

So, what happened?

After interviewing several people who passed by Bell at L'Enfant station that day, Weingarten concluded that it wasn't that people didn't have the capacity to understand the beauty of Bell's music, it wasn't that they weren't intelligent enough to recognize his talent, and it wasn't that they didn't *want* to stop and enjoy the music. People didn't stop to take it the performance because the music *wasn't relevant to them in the moment.*

In terms of marketing, this is a big lesson—*context* can be the difference between making $32 per hour and making *$60,000 per hour.*

Do I have your attention?

If you have attempted some content marketing on your own, and if you are frustrated with your results so far, this message is especially important for you. It's not that what you have to say isn't brilliant, needed, and important, and it's not that you aren't putting *enough* out there. It's likely that what you have provided so far is simply not relevant within the context it was shared.

Context is what sets the stage for people to take in and act on the information you're providing. Without it, just as Joshua Bell experienced, you are doomed for a "flop." As humans in this noisy world, we must *choose* where we expend our focus. As a result, if your audience doesn't immediately see the value of your content, or if they don't understand how to use it and what to focus on, they are going to simply do the easiest thing—nothing.

Which is exactly what happened to Joshua Bell.

So, how do you create context?

To create a context that will set your content up to win, you need three very important things, each of which are absolutely vital to your success. In fact, if any single one of these three factors is off, your potential rate of return will drastically diminish. You need:

the **right content**,
to the **right audience**,
at the **right time**.

1. THE RIGHT CONTENT

The right content is your "wow" factor. It's an empowering and useful message that leaves people wanting more. Again that doesn't mean it's heady, or dense, or massive. Your goal is not to create *a lot* of content, it's to create the "right" content.

The "right" content is something your clients *feel* and thank you for. It's on point, organized, practical and action-oriented. And at the same time, it is easy to understand, easy-to-digest and easy to enjoy. It is real, trustworthy, and personable. It gets people thinking, and concurrently gives them answers. In total, the "right" content is *simultaneously* both crystal clear and richly meaningful.

This may sounds like a lot, but it is completely within your grasp. It simply requires a bit of solid planning and a generous dose of authenticity.

It starts by creating a laser-like focus on what you really want, meaning the results you're hoping to accomplish by sending out a particular piece of content marketing. Perhaps you are looking for more quality leads, maybe you are launching a new product, or possibly you simply want to create a better connection with your audience. You will have to get super clear in order to create something worthwhile.

Next, ask yourself: What specific content strategies will help me accomplish *that result*?

Once you know what you are creating, look for ways to build out your content in a way that adds value to your clients or potential clients. In other words, decide on the specific type of excellence you are helping them achieve.

Then, get busy researching and/or creating proven strategies and tools that will them achieve that excellence. Focus on presenting action-oriented processes and steps that will incite both interest and follow-through. When they start to get results—and even the smallest of results *matter* to your audience—they'll be hooked with wanting more.

Lastly, and this is the one that most people miss—explain the "why" behind the strategies and tools you share. How will you explain to people why these are the best steps to take in achieving their specific form of excellence? What is the data *behind* your formula that explains why it really works?

Knowing how to share this information is paramount. In fact, the "why" is actually the most important part of the content you present because it is what will make it sustainable. If you know how to communicate the "why" behind your content, you will be able to tap into the emotion that becomes the basis for your audience to follow through. This is how you expand your reach and make the most of your efforts by adapting your content to a variety of different types of technology, as well as multiple marketing and distribution channels.

If you don't take the time to build out a plan for your content, you will be relegating yourself to the luck of the draw, without any of knowing for sure if you're going to get any results that will serve your business objectives. However, if you do take the time, you are likely have an immediate and direct impact on your margin of returns.

But that's not all you need.

2. THE RIGHT AUDIENCE

When Joshua Bell performed in L'Enfant Plaza, only one person out of the 1,070 who passed by actually recognized who he was… and that was not until the very end of his performance. Two of the seven people who stopped to listen had some violin or musical experience themselves. Although they didn't know they were listening to Joshua Bell, they were more apt to recognize his talent because they were the "right audience" for his work.

Knowing who will recognize and appreciate the value you have to provide is also essential to your marketing success. If you are not presenting it to the right audience, your message simply gets lost in the shuffle… where it will be overlooked, undervalued and simply ignored.

When Nike created its successful "Just Do It" campaign in 1988, it worked because the company made a notable shift in how they defined their *target audience*.

Prior to releasing the first "Just Do It" ad featuring Walt Stack, a then-80-year-old running icon, Nike had been focused on targeting elite or semi-elite athletes. Their previous campaigns provided research statistics and promises to make running shoes that would help elite athletes perform better.

But amid a market decline and company layoffs, in 1988, Nike decided to make a shift. Recognizing that fitness was becoming increasingly important to the popular at large, as baby boomers were starting to show interest in the need to stay in shape, Nike decided to start speaking to the average, out-of-shape person. They shifted their target audience from already fit and strong people to those who *wanted to be* that person. Nike started targeting the procrastinators out there, the people who were struggling with weight or health issues, the people who wanted to be fit, but who just wasn't quite there yet.

In this end, this somewhat simple shift in perspective created a 43 percent growth in Nike's sales over a 10-year period.

To get this kind of growth in your business, it starts by getting ridiculously clear about is who exactly your ideal audience is. As you do this, consider your audience using these two different approaches:

1 What are the facts about this audience? What are their *demographics*, which includes things like their gender, age range, income or financial status, education level, family situation, where they live, and interests or hobbies.

2 What is the psychology of your audience? What emotions do they experience that drive them? This is called their *psychographics*, which includes things like their hopes, fears, frustrations and dreams. What are the biggest problems that keep them up at night? If they could push a button and magically solve one problem, what would it be? What do they want their life to be like in a year?

These are questions you'll want to answer the best you can up front, but that you'll also continue to ponder and refine throughout the lifetime of your relationship with your audience.

Here's the moral of the story—deciding and then knowing *exactly* to whom you are speaking, and choosing that audience matters. A lot.

But to ensure your content marketing really works, there is one more factor you have to keep in mind, as well.

3. THE RIGHT TIME

Even if you have the perfect content and are sharing it with your exact target audience, it won't matter much if your timing is off.

Bad timing, in fact, was arguably the greatest factor contributing to Joshua Bell's "flop" performance in the subway. People were in such a hurry to get to their next destination, they didn't have the mental capacity necessary to take in the amazing gift he was offering. Many were too preoccupied, distracted, and focused on the objectives of their busy day to even really notice him.

Simply put—good timing creates a natural opening for a message that ensures it will simply be heard in the first place.

Back in 1995, you may remember a popular commercial featuring three frogs croaking in sequence: "Bud... bud... weis... bud... weis... bud... weis... bud... weis... er."

When creative professionals at D'Arcy Advertising first pitched this Budweiser "frogs" concept to Anheuser-Busch during an annual company planning meeting, there was a painful silence in the room.

Awkwardly and with his neck on the line, the account representative from D'Arcy was forced to make his pitch a second time.

Thankfully, about halfway through the repeated pitch, a few people began to smile, and by the end of the presentation, the entire room was laughing. The concept was so original, so different, and so... random when placed in a corporate environment that it had taken a moment to sink in.

But then August Busch III asked a key question: Where's it going to run?

The D'Arcy account representative responded quickly: "In position 1-A during the Super Bowl," he said. "That's the first thirty-second commercial break after the first possession in the first quarter. It will be the first commercial anyone sees."

As and it turned out, this timing was brilliant.

Unlike its original debut on cardboard, the Budweiser Frogs campaign immediately connected with its target audience, at exactly the *right moment*.

In fact, after the game, so many people remembered and appreciated the Frogs commercial that some analysts considered it to be even more memorable than the Super Bowl game itself.

The book, *Bitter Brew: The Rise and Fall of Anheuser-Busch and America's Kings of Beer* by William Knoedelseder explains:

"On January 29, 1995, quarterback Steve Young threw a record six touchdown passes to lead his San Francisco 49ers to a 49–26 victory over the San Diego Chargers in Super Bowl XXIX. But the real winning team that day may have been the Budweiser Frogs, who outscored even the legendary Spuds MacKenzie in *USA Today*'s weekly Ad Track poll, which measured the popularity and effectiveness of ad campaigns. Ad Track rated "Frogs" No. 1 for three months running, with more than 50 percent of poll respondents saying they recalled the commercial and liked it 'a lot.'"

As the old adage goes, "Timing is everything."

Had the Frogs commercial originally aired during a PBS special, mid-day during a soap opera, or perhaps simply just closer to the *end* of the Super Bowl game, the success of the response from the would likely have been different—not because people wouldn't like it, but because they may just not "get it" fast enough to create a meaningful response.

These three factors—the right content, the right audience, and the right timing—will take you to the Shangri-La of content marketing, i.e., that sweet spot where the energy you put in is compounded into noteworthy results.

I invite you to take a step back to look at your content marketing efforts objectively up to this point: What have been the results of all your content marketing efforts so far?

Although creating context is not necessarily *easy*, it *is* much easier than blinding churning out mass quantities of information that are not really garnering the results you crave.

In what ways may you currently be working too hard on content production? Where are you spinning your wheels with little to no results?

Is your content currently shared within a context that is working? And if not, how can you make it better?

CHAPTER TWO: THE BIG TAKE-AWAY

Taking the time to craft the right message, for the right audience, at the right time will enable you will be able to act with purpose, work less, and get the most out of your content marketing efforts.

"

The way customers relate to brands and how profit is generated has changed so dramatically, almost every professional is being challenged to reconsider what they do in order to stay relevant.

—Simon Mainwaring

CHAPTER 2: RESOURCES

To improve the relevance of your content marketing techniques and ensure you are delivering it under the "right" context, try asking yourself the following questions:

1   What is the ultimate end-result I would like to achieve with my content marketing efforts?

2   What specific content strategies will help me accomplish *that result*?

3   What information will help my clients and potential clients achieve the specific kind of excellence they crave?

4   What steps, tools and strategies will make their journey to excellence easy, clear and productive?

5   What are the core principles behind all of the steps, tools and strategies I provide? *Why* do they work?

6   Who will recognize and appreciate the value I have to offer?

7   How can I package my information to make it easy to consume and understand, while reinforcing my company's core brand values?

8   At what time of day, time of week, and time of year will my clients and potential clients be open to receiving the insight and wisdom I have to offer?

CHAPTER THREE
HELLO? CAN YOU HEAR ME?

"Marketing is a contest for people's attention."
—*Seth Godin*

I have some potentially shocking news for you—click-through rates may not be the best way to measure your marketing performance.

Because we are living in the era of click-to-like, click-to-love, and click-to-buy, this may seem like a radical statement.

And don't get me wrong—click-throughs *are* a good statistic to follow and track. They definitely give you some great (and immediate) intel about how well your content is being received online. Click-throughs rates do tell you overall if your audience is liking the vibe of what you are putting out there, and most important, if it's compelling enough to get them to act.

However, the click-through rate concept is a bit flawed in that it doesn't necessarily confirm that those who "clicked" actually read, watched, or listened to your content. In fact, there is a great article in *Time* by Tony Haile entitled, *What You Think You Know About the Web Is Wrong.*

This article provides some interesting statistics that challenge the way we typically think about online experiences. In short, here are the top take-aways:

Myth 1: We read what we click on.

Reality: Fewer than 55 percent of people spend more than 15 seconds actively on a page.

Myth 2: We read what we share.

Reality: Extensive studies show that most people share social media content without actually engaging with the information themselves.

Myth 3: People read the top (i.e. banners) of a page first.

Reality: 66% of the attention on a normal page is spent below the fold. People now assume that a banner is an ad of some kind, so they scroll past the top until they find the actual content.

Source: "What You Think You Know About the Web Is Wrong," Tony Haile, *Time*, March 9, 2014. Statistical data by: Tony Haile—Chartbeat

As content marketers, what does all this data mean?

First of all, it's clear that the click-through rate is no longer *the measure* of online performance. It is a measurement, and a pretty solid one at that, however it's not the only one. And, as the stats above illustrate, it's no longer the most important statistic for you to watch.

Which leads to the question—what is?

When it comes to content, where your outcome is to build *relationships* that convert to sales, you want to be tracking something a bit deeper, which is this—*attention*.

Attention, *real attention*, is the prelude to a relationship. It means that someone actually read, listened to, or viewed your content. And if that is true, they are more likely to want more… which is the kind of valuable lead that may soon convert into a sale.

In content marketing, your goal is much more than clicks and "likes." You are taking clients through a process, and with each step they take in their journey for excellence, you are building an increasing level of trust with them.

In total, there are five key stages of connection, each one requiring a deeper level of content absorption by your clients:

 5 STAGES OF A CONTENT MARKETING RELATIONSHIP

1 Attraction

2 Engagement

3 Brand Immersion

4 Follow Up & Implementation

5 Ongoing Mastery & Leadership

So often we just think about content marketing as just one big hook. In fact, most content marketers spend about 90 percent of their time solely concentrated on the "attraction" stage at the beginning of the funnel, and forget to consider the bigger picture down the road... However, this is where you will make the largest impact (and glean the greatest pay-back).

"

Be careful not to sacrifice long-term profits
for short-term gain.

—John Reese

In short, if you want your content to transition from simple clicks and "likes" to actual sales and further long-term engagement in your business, you are going to need to start focusing on ways you can hold your prospects' attention for much longer.

Interestingly, the same researchers at Chartbeat who uncovered the data about how many people actually read what they click on or share confirmed this priority. They found that if you can hold a visitor's attention for as little as three minutes, they are *twice as likely* to return to seek more content from you, then if you had only held their attention for one minute.

So, how can you get (and keep) your prospects' attention for longer?

There are six ways.

1. SHARE CONTENT THAT IS RELEVANT.

Since I love content, I subscribe to several different blogs, news providers, and content producers. But like everyone else, my time is valuable, and I don't have time to read absolutely everything that comes into my in-box. So, I have created a set of rules to help me determine what is read-worthy... and it's kind of a tall order.

For me to read it, the content has to:

- be a clear and practical use of my time

- have immediate value, meaning it solves an urgent problem I am working in the moment

- hit my in-box at just the right moment when I am open, interested, and/or simply curious

In other words, for me to engage in content (even though I love it and want to read it all), the information has to be *highly relevant to me, in the immediate moment.*

Now, obviously you will never know what is going on with each of your clients and prospects in every moment of every day to be able to fulfill these requirements on an everyday basis. However, if you make an effort to genuinely put yourself in their shoes and to really consider the problems and frustrations your prospects may be facing each day, you are much more likely to create the kind of relevant content needed to grab their attention and draw them in.

2. SHARE CONTENT THAT IS NEW.

Behavioral scientists have done the research—as humans, we like things that are *new*.

As the 18th century writer and politician, Joseph Addison, explains:

"Everything that is new or uncommon raises a pleasure in the imagination, because it feels the soul with an agreeable surprise, gratifies its curiosity, and gives it an ideas of which it was not before possessed."

The same is true in the 21st century. Just go to Apple.com and start counting how many times you see the word "new" in their marketing copy. (It's a lot.)

As underwhelmingly complex as it seems, simply adding a starburst or label that showcases that your content as "new" can be the difference between an actual read and an empty click.

Note: Be sure that what you call "new" actually is in some way—be authentic. However, this doesn't mean that you can only brand *original* content with the "new" tag. For example, a content refresh can be described as a "new edition." Or, you might have a "new" perspective to share regarding an already existing topic.

3. SHARE CONTENT THAT EVOKES STRONG EMOTION.

Emotions (especially those that are positive) are a powerful way to quickly draw in and hold a person's attention.

As an example, I'd like to share yet another Budweiser commercial that aired during a more recent Super Bowl. (If you've been following my content for very long, you probably already know, I am an avid football fan!)

This commercial starts off by introducing us to a sweet, yellow Labrador Retriever puppy who pops his head out of a bale of hay to greet both his owner and a giant Clydesdale in a neighboring stall. With a bold and curious expression on his adorable face, he bounds past his owner and out the barn door behind his owner's back. However, because the Clydesdale is facing the opposite direction, he sees the puppy leave and lets out a concerned whimper as he exits. The puppy then jumps in an empty horse trailer and gets a ride to town. And as the trailer comes to stop, he manages to jump out and run down the street… getting even further away from home.

Next, we see the owner, who is, by the way, a ruggedly handsome man, who is now in distress, posting flyers about a "Lost Puppy." And then we see the puppy cowering in a cardboard box during a rainstorm. Meanwhile, both the owner and the Clydesdale are becoming increasingly upset.

The puppy travels though fields and forests and somehow manages to make his way back to a hilltop overlooking his home and barn. And then… the Clydesdale spots him through a gap in the wood paneling.

Dirty and scared, the puppy is so close to finding his way home. But suddenly, a menacing, growling wolf encroaches on him from behind. The puppy starts to whimper… and then… the barn doors break open.

Four giant Clydesdale horses burst out of the barn, breaking through their stall doors to stampede to his rescue, forming a line of protection behind him. Just then music is cued—a heartfelt remake of "Less than Jake" by The Pretenders… "I would walk 500 miles, and I would walk 500 more, just to be the man who walked 1,000 miles, to fall down at your door."

The puppy is saved. Clydesdales and puppy are reunited.

And then the horses lead the puppy back to reunite him with his stunningly relieved and grateful owner, as well… who celebrates by slinging back a Budweiser beer. As the music fades, the screen graphic transitions in close to: "Budweiser #BestBuds"

I used the example of this commercial in one of my presentations, and when I showed it to my 6-foot-plus tall, tough husband to test it out, it brought tears.

So, why does Budweiser do this? Beer and puppies don't necessarily have anything in common. At face value, this was a very roundabout way to encourage people to drink more Budweiser.

But the executives at Anheuser Busch and the smart ad agency, Anomaly, who created this ad, know that if you can capture an audience emotively, you will have secured their absolute and undivided attention.

They know we will all remember something that creates raw, real *emotion*.

But, you don't have to be a big brand like Budweiser to do this. And you don't have to use puppies. You just need to think about how your message can uniquely trigger positive emotions for your audience.

To start, here are some of the most influential universal themes you could include: love, justice, altruism, courage, and awe.

The bottom line is scientists know for a fact that we feel first and think second. They've determined that our sensory brain—the part of our brain that really responds to, feels, experiences and acts on emotion—responds to things in one-fifth of the amount of time as our cognitive brain—the part of our brain that thinks.

In other words, we are hard-wired as human beings to react, look out for, respond to, take in and act on emotion more than anything else we experience. The stronger the emotion you can evoke in your audience with your content and marketing, the better result you'll get from it.

 PAIN VS. POSITIVITY

You may be thinking, "But wait! Isn't pain a more powerful motivator?" The answer to this question is yes; it just depends on the timing. When you first meet someone you don't want to make them feel lousy, you want them to associate positive emotions to you and your business. When it comes time for the sale, however, this is when you want to start tapping into your prospect's deepest pain and bring it to the surface, so he or she is motivated to act.

4. SHARE CONTENT THAT STIMULATES VISUAL SENSES.

Researchers are constantly working to figure out all of the nuances corresponding to positive consumer responses. But it's tricky...

because as soon as they figure it a formula for success, either the technology changes or people change their behavior. This is yet another consequence of living in a world where such a vast amount of content is constantly revealed.

However, there is one factor that has stood out throughout multiple studies over the course of time—people respond to *visual* stimuli.

In fact, the data consistently reveals that content including some type of visual elements converts more than any other medium. In most cases, content that includes a photograph, and illustration, or a graphic will be consumed and shared more often than those that don't.

Knowing this fact, it would behoove you to include visuals in your marketing messages. They don't have to be polished and perfect—just mix it up and make them feel authentic.

For example, sometimes I will post a professional-looking image with a quote on Facebook, or other times, I might share a photo of a handwritten quote in my journal with me pointing to it or a picture of me totally disheveled after making a mistake related to the topic. It's the same content message, but the visual variety makes it interesting, and interesting is what creates traction.

5. SHARE CONTENT THAT IS PERSONALIZED.

If you can make your content connect with people in a personal way, they are much more likely to engage with your message. And there are *a lot* of ways to do this—beyond simply coding your emails to include the first name of each recipient.

For example, I like to send out hand-written cards and gifts to my top clients. I genuinely enjoy doing this, and it forces me to take the time to think about each individual person. Obviously, I can't do this with *all* of my clients and prospects, but for those who are more deeply immersed in my brand, it's a great way to further the relationship.

Another option is to send out a survey. When you engage clients in an authentic dialogue, that's personalization.

Or, you could provide access for certain special customers to insider information. Rewarding top tier clients makes them rewards them for their loyalty and lets them know they are important, known, and appreciated by you.

Lastly, one of my favorite examples of personalized marketing is Office Depot's "Elf Yourself" campaign. If you go to elfyourself. com, you will guided through an easy process to upload yours and up to four friends' faces into an app where you can place them onto the bodies of a group of happy, zany dancing elves.

This creates a little JibJab-esque video that you can forward to friends or post on social media. To ensure marketing benefits, the landing page where you create your video, as well as the link sent both have subtle, but clearly labeled links to, "Shop OfficeDepot. com Now."

This is brilliant, and there is nothing preventing you from doing something like this for your audience. Your goal is simply to enable people to make themselves part of your engagement, to help them feel like they are invested in and part of content shared, and encourage them to contribute to your message overall.

6. SHARE CONTENT THAT CREATES SURPRISE.

The odds are good that you have seen the 2009 episode of *Britain's Got Talent* featuring Susan Boyle.

It went something like this.

Susan comes on stage, looking a little older and less glamorous than those whom we traditionally think of as performers, and Simon Cowell asks her flatly, "Okay, what's the dream?"

"I'm trying to be a professional singer," Boyle replies.

"And why hasn't it worked out so far, Susan?" Cowell counters.

"I have never been given the chance before, but here's hoping it will all change."

At this point, Cowell kind of raises an eyebrow and the audience looks a little bit terrified for her, but the judges tell her to proceed.

And then she opens her mouth. After a single phrase, the crowd begins cheering. Her voice is *that good.* And the surprise of so much unexpected beauty coming such a humble, seemingly average person… is absolutely breathtaking.

I never get tired of watching this video.

I will engage with this content over and over again even though I *know* the surprise that's coming. But I do so because the message is so meaningful.

This type of surprise reminds us all what we're capable of. When we see just a normal person like us doing something extraordinary that they are unsure about, it's creates an inspiring mental flip that turns on something inside of *us*.

If you can do *that* with your content marketing—if you can use case studies about your own best clients to create surprise success stories, you will have new prospects hooked, and ready to engage at the next level.

This, like all of the other strategies I just shared, doesn't require a ton of legwork or research to implement. You don't have to do an in-depth study to find out what people are into, or come up with unbelievably out-of-the-box ideas to get people's attention.

You simply need to pay attention to your own clients. Get to know them. Think about the stage of relationship you are currently in. Take notice of what they are talking about, and use the principles outlined in this chapter to guide you in a targeted approach for new content.

If you *pay attention to them* long enough, they are going to do some pretty amazing things that will help direct your efforts in figuring out how to best get *them to pay attention you.*

CHAPTER THREE: THE BIG TAKE-AWAY

As a content marketer, the most important data-point you *can measure is your effectiveness in holding your audience's attention.* By using proven principles for increasing the attention rate of content consumers, a prospect is more likely to enter into a deeper stage of a relationship with you, as opposed to simply being a "one-click-wonder."

CHAPTER 3: RESOURCES

Because they are your first opportunity to capture someone's attention, your headlines are important. Challenge yourself to improve your headline-writing skills. Here are some guidelines to help you create headlines that hook:

1 Use numbers.

Example: "47 Ways to…" "47 Known Ways to…" or "47 Sure-Fire Ways to…"

2 Avoid superlatives or hyperbole.

3 Use "you" and "your."

Example: "Do You…?" (i.e. "Do You Make These Mistakes?")

4 Be clear about who it's for.

5 Highlight benefits.

Examples: "Here's a Method That's Helping _____ People to _____" or "Here's a Quick Way to…"

6 Capitalize the first letter of each word.

7 Be ultra specific and direct.

Example: "How to…" or "How to… Even If…"

8 Inspire intrigue.

Example: "Why Some People…"

9 Use urgency.

Example: "Now or Never…" or "The First 22 People Only…"

> **"**
>
> *I am one who believes that one of the greatest dangers of advertising is not that of misleading people, but that of boring them to death.*
>
> *—Leo Burnett*

CHAPTER FOUR
IT'S NOT ABOUT YOU, BUT IT IS

"The greatest good you can do for another is not just to share your riches but to reveal to him his own."
—Benjamin Disraeli

When he was in the 4th grade, my youngest son, Ben had to write a special end-of-the-year report about a famous person from California, where we live.

Immediately, Ben selected the famous 49ers quarterback, Joe Montana, from his teacher's list of possible candidates. The only catch was this—in order to secure their choices, students in his class had to "apply" for their selection. And unfortunately, Ben was home sick for a few days during the week when other kids were securing some of the most coveted selections.

So, in order to get his unequivocal top pick, Ben was going to have to take it a step further by writing something especially compelling to *convince* his teacher the he was *the best kid* to win the bid for Joe Montana on his selection bid.

As he sat down to write his application letter and told me about his predicament, he piqued my curiosity, and so I asked him a few questions that I thought might help him craft a persuasive letter.

"Ben," I said, "Why do you want to do your report on Joe Montana?"

"Well, I love football. And I want to play football when I grow up, so I want to know what it's like," he replied.

I push him a little further: "But why is this so important to you?"

"I want to know the trouble he went through to get his dream so I can get my dream," he says.

Proudly I think to myself—great answer for a nine-year-old! But, I still push him a little further and ask another question, "Buddy, this is all great in terms of what it's going to give you and why you want to do this report so badly. I love your passion, but I've got to ask, what's in it for *other* people? Why would *other people* want to hear your report on Joe Montana? What would it do for them?"

This same question is something I often find myself asking clients, as well.

It's a simple concept and is something we all know is important rationally, but when get excited about our own passion or stuck in the details of a product or service, it's easy to get lost in our own story. Whether it is the pressure of delivery in looking for something to say, or simply human nature that gives us pleasure in talking about ourselves, we forget that the reason we are sharing the information with someone else in the first place is to improve *their* life in some way.

This is especially true of a "signature talk," that is the entry-point presentation that summarizes a thought leader's core message, while emphasizing the key value he or she brings to the table. Whether you own your own business or work for someone else, you are more than likely familiar with this concept, even if you call it something else.

However, in my experience, although *most* people understand the concept of a signature talk, they don't really know *how* to do. In as many as 99 percent of the signature talks I have heard, the speakers and presenters on stage didn't know how to tell their core story in a way that emphasized their audience's needs, not theirs.

Initially, this does seem like a somewhat tricky outcome—you are endeavoring to tell a story that is about yourself, but not *really* about yourself.

Here's what I mean.

When I asked Ben that question, "What would it do for *other people* to hear your report on Joe Montana," he thought about it for a minute or so, and here is what is said:

"Well… so I can help others understand football better so they can learn to appreciate the sport. So maybe if they don't like football, I can help them change their opinion and see the good things it does. Like my coach tells me, it builds teamwork and leadership."

As a mom, and I was beyond impressed with this response, and could not believe that it was coming from my wise-beyond-his-years son.

That is real value that would definitely benefit the audience.

Even so, I push him one more time, "So how is your report going to *help* your audience," I asked.

At this point, Ben started to get excited, and I saw a twinkle appear in his eye, "Mom, maybe if I show how hard Joe Montana worked to get his dream, it'll make other people want to work to get their dreams!"

Boom.

I could not have been more proud.

It was a small shift in focus that would end up having a huge impact on his audience.

That is the power of asking questions... which is something I challenge you do with yourself in creating, or improving upon your signature talk.

So, how do you do it?

Here are five keys to building a successful signature talk:

 HOW TO BUILD A SIGNATURE TALK

1 Open with a personal story.

2 Know where your talk is going and what you want it to do.

3 Position yourself as the person who can solve their problem.

4 Don't over-teach!

5 Build toward the one offer (paid or not).

1. OPEN WITH A PERSONAL STORY.

When I first started doing presentations, I would come out on stage and do what I've seen a lot of other speakers do. I would thank the audience for being there and for having me. I would thank the promoters for the opportunity to be there. Then, I would thank the hotel and the crew for their hospitality in creating such a great environment.

None of this genuinely connected with my audience. And none of it was really relevant to what I had to share.

After a couple of years delivering my intro this way, my good friend and master storyteller, Bo Eason, called me out.

I had a really powerful story about my mom that I would close my talks with, and at the end of a presentation Bo attended, he came up to me and said, "Pam, that story you tell at the end is so powerful emotionally. You really had the audience's full attention—why aren't you leading with *that*?"

Good question.

After I made this change by putting an emotive and *real* story upfront, at the very start of my presentation, it created a huge improvement in terms in how well I could relate to and therefore, how well I could impact and influence my audience.

So, learn from my mistake—lead with your personal story but make sure it has a key take-away or lesson that's meaningful. Trust me, there's nothing worse than a presenter who tells a story that's clearly for their own benefit and edification, even if it's not their intent.

A good signature talk takes people on a journey. It puts them in a position where they can see, feel, and experience *your journey*, so that they can imagine what life would be like on the other side *for them*.

In content marketing, your signature talk is the description of your pathway to excellence, and it describes how to achieve that same version of excellence for your audience in a way that's meaningful to them.

You share where you were when you first started... which is likely exactly where most of them are right now. You explain the pains you went through... which are most likely the fears and concerns they are currently experiencing. And then you explain how you broke through and got to where you are now... giving them faith and trust that you will be able to lead them to victory, as well.

This creates an emotional connection with both new and experienced audiences because all of a sudden, they see you as a *real* human being, and as someone they can relate to. What's more—they see you as an *imperfect* being, which gives them an even deeper connection to you. Just as we all felt more connected to Susan Boyle after we saw her overcome the preconceived notions about her, as well as her own doubts and fear, a good signature talk creates compassion and connection in a similar way. (And in fact, a really great signature talk will incorporate all six attention-grabbing strategies—relevance, new-ness, strong emotion, visual stimulation, personalization, and surprise.)

Remember your "story" is a transformational experience to which your audience will be able to relate. You are recanting how you successfully arrived at a point of excellence they desire, while humbly relating to where they are right now by sharing the honest roadblocks, fears, and difficulties you experienced along the way. This will give your audience an opportunity to experience you in a more personal way.

In addition, starting with your story often has the added bonus of getting you out of head and into your heart, so that you can more easily express your authentic personality during your presentation.

However, in doing all of this, don't forget that the average person's attention span is about eight seconds. And with this in mind, be careful as you create the timing, sequencing, and pace of your story, Choose your first words wisely, and make sure your opening statement is as succinct, clear, and captivating as possible.

2. KNOW WHERE YOUR TALK IS GOING AND WHAT YOU WANT IT TO DO.

As a speaker, you can use your talk to close sales at the end of your presentation because throughout the presentation, you are naturally seeding little messages about what makes you different and unique, while emphasizing why your brand is so valuable between the lines. It's not that you are even trying to sell, it's just that your signature talk, if authentic and relatable, will make the right audience desire your advice or support in getting to the next level.

It can also you accomplish what's called a "tripwire," or introductory sale. The idea is that if you can get someone to raise their hand and commit to investing in a lower priced item during your signature presentation, they are much more likely to invest in future products and services down the road.

In addition, a good signature talk will likely also serve to position you in your field and may even stimulate requests for additional future speaking engagements. Promoters are always looking for experts and authorities in a particular area, and having a signature talk more clearly positions you as a thought leader in a specific, targeted field.

Even it if just a small next step to purchase a strategy session or a book, your signature talk should be leading your audience to *do something*.

So, plan for this—know where you are taking people and what sale you want to make afterwards, and weave this into your presentation, artfully. It's not an in-your-face sales pitch, rather you are simply connecting people to great solutions (i.e., your products and services) that will help solve their problems.

3. POSITION YOURSELF AS THE PERSON WHO CAN SOLVE THEIR PROBLEM.

Throughout your talk, use purposeful sub-stories to position yourself as a thought leader and trusted advisor in your field. You are the expert people can come to get the results they desire.

While doing so, be clear about what *type of person* will get the best results from you, and then make a point to speak directly to *that person*.

Your goal is not to convert every person in the audience to a paying customer; your goal is capture *quality leads* and make *quality sales* to those customers who will genuinely benefit from your product or service. These are the people with whom you will want to invest in to establish an ongoing relationship, as they are more apt to become your long-term clients.

Your signature talk should create consistency in your messaging. Nothing will kill your ability to build a brand more than being all over the place. Since the majority presenters tend to focus on creating multiple presentations, they easily end up making this mistake. And as a result, message clarity and constancy are often sadly underrated in many introductory presentations.

However, this shortsighted trend can actually create a great opportunity for you. If you break from the crowd and take the time to create a presentation that pinpoints the problems your expertise solves *from your audience's vantage point*, it will separate you from competitors, drive your market to pay attention to what *you* have to say, and ultimately entice people to want to do business with you.

4. DON'T OVER-TEACH!

This is a big one for me that was hard to learn.

I have so much passion for helping my clients succeed that I used to try to pack my signature talk to the brim with an abundance of tips, techniques, and resources. I wanted to give the audience absolutely everything I had, in every single delivery.

And because I really wanted to get my speaking legs under me and felt that I needed the practice, I went out and worked to book *a lot* of speaking engagements. And I thought I had to do a different talk for every, single unique audience. I also figured I needed to share a lot of detailed information to add substantive value.

Although virtuous and well-intentioned, this strategy easily backfired. I learned that people need space and time to absorb each part of my message, and that too much data all at one time is actually a turn-off. Plus, since they felt over-satiated and almost even burdened by the objectives provided, an overwhelmed audience would rarely take action after my talks.

Knowing what I do now, if I could have just taken the same time to create one solid signature talk focused on just a couple key points, and then used that same presentation with slightly different framing and formatting to speak successfully to each of those audiences. It would have saved me a lot of time and been much more valuable for the audience.

Remember, a confused person does the easiest thing—nothing.

So focus on just sharing two or three of your best ideas in your signature talk. Choose relatively simple concepts that they can use right away to help. In doing so, you'll leave them feeling both excited about what is possible and hungry for more.

Planning your presentation this way takes the pressure off of you, and it actually makes your talk more enjoyable for your audience, as well.

In addition, this allows you focus your time on building your list, going after new audiences, and nurturing relationships—instead of on creating multiple new talks.

5. BUILD TOWARD THE ONE OFFER (PAID OR NOT).

Use the rest of your presentation to build toward your close by asking the audience to take *one* clear and simple next step. Don't ask them to do multiple things, or give them options.

Instead, tell them the *one thing* they can do right now to get bigger and better results form working you with you, such as a free consultation, a product, or a "next level" program.

When complete and effective, your signature talk is something you can share with *anyone, anywhere.* It's something you can use over and over again to connect with new audiences, so you don't have to constantly reinvent the wheel with a new talk for each gig. In fact, you will want to use a version of it at the front end of almost everything you do—including speaking engagements, webcast presentations, webinars, and/or written publications.

You also have to remember to *keep telling your story...* even as you become more advanced in your field. One of the things big companies are struggling with in today's hyper-connected world is how to take their brand back down to the personal. Many have grown so large that they've forgotten their roots and have become disassociated with the core, relatable values that originally made them relatable to their audience.

If this all seems like a lot to you, take a step back and relax. The last big piece of advice I can tell you about creating this powerful marketing tool is this—don't overthink it!

After all is said and done, a signature talk is simply a raw, real, authentic representation of *you* and what you have to offer. And if you enjoy creating it, your audience will enjoy receiving it.

CHAPTER FOUR: THE BIG TAKE-AWAY

A great signature talk is a captivating and engaging multi-purpose story that explains to audiences the distinct and relatable value you offer, how it will benefit them, and why you are the right person to partner with on their journey. Taking the time to strategically craft your signature talk has many benefits that will save you time and increase your sale-ability.

"

I'm going to make a long speech because I've not had the time to prepare a short one.

—*Winston Churchill*

 **CHAPTER 4: RESOURCES**

To further build upon or refine your signature talk, try asking yourself the following questions:

1 Ultimately, why do you want to share this content?

2 Why is this topic important to you?

3 Why would *other people* want to hear about this topic?

4 How does your topic solve *their core problem(s)*?

5 What have you personally overcome to achieve this core desire of your audience?

6 What story can you tell about your own life to showcase the most challenging aspects of your journey that helped you get where you are today?

7 What does your story provide for other people? What are the lessons they can glean from your journey?

8 How would it *help* other people to hear your story?

9 What are the most emotive aspects of your story, and how can you use them to better relate to your audience?

10 What is *one offer* you can make that would benefit your audience the most?

CHAPTER FIVE
THE (CONTENT) CIRCLE OF LIFE

"If a seed of a lettuce will not grow, we do not blame the lettuce. Instead, the fault lies with us for not having nourished the seed properly."
—*Buddhist Proverb*

2,085 exabytes.

That's how much digital data is estimated to be out there now in the world-wide-web today.

And if you don't know what an exabyte is, I don't really either!. All I can tell you is that it is a very large number. One exabyte is the equivalent of about one billion gigabytes.

With so much data already out there, it may seem daunting imagining how content generators come up with totally original, new ideas... all the time.

Let me in on a little secret. We don't.

With so much data already out there, our job as content creators is not to invent breakthrough new data, to conduct major studies, or to discover lost civilizations. In fact, excessive focus on theory over practical application will often work against you when it comes to marketing.

Our job is simply to do three things:

THE 3 STAGES OF CONTENT DEVELOPMENT

1 Curate

2 Architect

3 Produce

1. CURATING CONTENT

The number one objection I get when people come to me for help with content usually goes something like this:

"But I'm not really an expert. I don't have any new content," or "But, I don't know how to come up with good content," or "But, my content isn't unique or special."

You get the idea.

When people first start creating content they often get stuck on this feeling that they have to create brand new raw data from scratch. But that's not really what makes our role in the world of information sharing helpful and meaningful to our clients.

As content marketers, the world appreciates the wisdom we share because it provides a way to understand and *apply* all the vast amounts of data out there.

We are *curators* of content. We discover, assimilate, and structure content. We figure out new ways to make it more relevant, more valuable, and more practical.

Just as a journalist does not *create* the news he or she writes, but rather collects the data and broadcasts it in a comprehensive way, content creators research, review, and reflect upon the existing data out there to synthesize it in useful ways.

We compare and contrast data to find connections, fallacies, or paradoxes. We apply data to our own lives and then share our personal experiences so others can learn from our successes and failures. We take the best of related ideas and put them together, enabling people to quickly learn how to master complex topics. And these are just a examples of content curation. There are many, many ways to apply this useful skill.

Here is a more standard definition:

 Content Curation: the process of collecting, organizing and displaying information relevant to a particular topic or area of interest.

Back in 2007 when the last big study of its kind was conducted, humans were broadcasting enough information for *each of us* to read 174 newspapers per day. Now the data in each of these newspapers would not necessarily be new and noteworthy in and of itself. However, what *is* interesting and unique is the style, perspective, and angle used in sharing each piece of information.

So, stop stressing about finding something so new to share that it's not even yet Google-able. Your goal is not to recreate the wheel, or to become the most knowledgeable person in your market.

In fact, simply knowing more than anyone else in your field will not get you very far. Your audience doesn't care if you are some super brainy wizard. They aren't coming to you because they think of you as a living encyclopedia. They are coming to you because you are human person they can relate to who is able to share quality information in a way they can appreciate, understand, and employ.

Here are five ways you can do this...

1. Share content as is

Save your clients time by finding the most useful, pertinent, and high-quality information related to your field for them. Most of us have to go through a lot of information to figure out what's good and what's not.

Therefore, if someone we respect provides us with something good, we appreciate it because it saves us a ton of research time. And a result of help in gifting us back some of our time, you become a trusted advisor.

Just be sure to properly credit any sources and be sure to follow copyright laws so you are sharing 3rd party information appropriately.

2. Provide perspective

No one has walked your shoes. No one has had the unique experiences you have had in your niche. And ultimately, people aren't paying you for what you know. They're paying you for your *perspective* on what you know.

People want to know what mistakes have you made, so they can learn from those mistakes and don't have to make them. They want your fresh take on old concepts. They want to know what shortcuts you use to get things done more efficiently. They want *your personal* recipe for success.

3. Aggregate

Create something useful or provide a new way of looking at data by collecting other people's research, and assimilating it into something new.

This is sort of what Tripadvisor does—they provide a space to showcase and rate all of the best hotels, restaurants, and entertainment providers out there. Then, they make it easy for fellow travelers to share their personal experiences at each of these establishments.

And because this useful aggregation of data, travelers can now easily access quality information that we used to have to search for on literally thousands of different individual sites.

This is also how most infographics are created. They work, not because they provide "new" data, but rather because they are aggregation of content put together in a visually stimulating way to prove a point, provide a new vantage point, or simplify a subject matter.

4. Provide access

Use your existing connections (or create new ones) to provide your clients with access to other experts in related fields. This is essentially what Maria Forleo did to turn her video blog into an extremely profitable online business school.

From a more traditional perspective, it's also what Barbara Walters is most famous for. She was able to provide us with access to some of the world's most interesting people and get them to share some of their most interesting thoughts and insights as related to popular current events.

You can do the same thing.

For example, if your area of expertise is weight loss, you could look for 20 of the best weight-loss specialists out there and ask them to share just one tip on how to lose weight. Then, you could showcase all 20 tips together, putting a byline next to each one to ensure you give each resource credit. When complete, you would have an awesome piece of content entitled, "20 Tips from the Top 20 Weight-Loss Experts."

Again, you did not come up with each of these tips yourself. However, the content ends up being potentially even more rich, credible, and meaningful than if you had tried to do so. Again, by taking the time to put together and provide access to this type of valuable information, your clients see you as a trusted adviser and indispensable content provider.

5. Distill data

Distilling data means to break down a lot of information and to then organize it into an easier to understand format.

CliffsNotes is a good example. Now featured digitally online, these smartly truncated book summaries were originally called *Cliff's Notes* and printed in little black and yellow books, saving students around the world from having to actually read every word of every book prescribed by their literature teachers.

Similarly, you distill information almost every time you post on Twitter by breaking the data down to just 140 characters.

To distill data is to give us the bottom line and the key take-aways. It is the big picture that people will ultimately want to remember after experiencing a larger, more in-depth piece of content.

You could even distill data by providing an overview of this book to your audience. If you wrote up a short blog or filmed a quick video entitled, "6 Practical Things I Learned from *The Art of Impact* by Pam Hendrickson," I don't mind because it makes me look good. And it also makes *you* look good because it features your lessons and insights.

Get the idea?

And so, as you continue your content marketing journey, start thinking of yourself as a content curator. This is a vital and needed role in the world of information today. And the sky is the limit in terms of what you can create and share.

2. ARCHITECTING CONTENT

To start building your content, you need two things: First a framework, meaning a unifying concept that everything is tied to, and then the parts that make up the framework.

Let's start with the framework.

Most people approach content development in a linear fashion. In grade school, most of learn that the first step in writing a report, paper, article, script, or story-board is to start with this thing called an *outline*.

First you come up with one big take-away your want your audience to walk away with. Then you build up supporting sub-points underneath that. Then, for each of those sub-points you come up with supporting details and more sub-points, and then more sub-sub points under that, etcetera, etcetera.

Although this type of linear approach is fine for school papers where you want to impress your teacher with how much you know, when applied to the world of content marketing, it can be one of the fastest and most effective ways to overwhelm your audience.

Here's why—the problem with traditional outlines is that they inherently encourage you to keep adding more, and more, and more.

If you want to structure content so that it's accessible and people really use it, you have to break it down into as few parts as possible.

And in a world where consumers are constantly looking for brevity and convenience, I propose that there is another way to organize your content that may get you a better result.

Here's how it works.

1   Start with your theme or idea.

2   Brainstorm all of your ideas around this topic. Sometimes it helps to create a circle in the middle of a page and to create branches that stem from the middle. I'm a visual person, so this works for me!

3   Review all that you've captured, and start circling all of the ideas related to one concept. When you're finished finding

your first set of related ideas, you will combine those ideas to create your first key point.

4 Then, repeat the process as many times as needed to define your additional key points.

5 After considering all the key points you've identified, select the top three that will make the most impact on your audience.

6 Ask yourself what sequence and framing will support the core topics you selected.

This is a great way to train yourself to think. So often we approach content as a building process, instead of more organically and directive, which helps you more strategically pinpoint the precise messaging needed to deliver your outcome, while giving your audience something substantive that they can get their arms around.

So, now that you have the content framework, you need to build out the parts, and from a content marketing standpoint, that often involves breaking ideas down into steps people can use to obtain their own results.

Here is one of my favorite strategies for creating step-by-step content:

1 Find a real person who would like to learn the content you are going to share.

2 Turn on your iPhone or other dictation-recording device.

3 Walk this person through the process, while capturing it on your recorder.

4 Go back and write down the key steps you shared. You can even transcribe the recording, and then simply edit the copy for a final piece.

In addition, here are 9 other great ways to create a framework for your content:

 9 CONTENT FRAMEWORKS

1   Categories or Lists

2   Principles / Rules / Laws / Habits

3   Common Mistakes (do's vs. don'ts)

4   Problems / Solutions

5   Storylines

6   Series of stories and/or case studies

7   Q&A segments or categorized questions

8   Model-based framework (uses diagrams based on triangles, systems, or funnels to showcase content)

9   Circular-based framework (uses organic, network-based diagrams such as mind-maps to showcase content)

Overall, efficiently and effectively architecting great content is something that simply requires practice. The more you create, the easier it will get.

3. PRODUCING CONTENT.

As a content marketer, the ability to turn and produce great content quickly is essential. When tasked with creating a high volume of ongoing content, it is common to get trapped in this mindset of content chaos, where you feel consumed by a weight on your shoulders to relentlessly produce something for Facebook, something for a blog, something for a podcast, and something for your YouTube channel all the same time.

But, the intentionality behind each piece of content shared still must remain a constant. You don't want to start creating what my friend Karen calls, "random acts of marketing," or you'll lose the credibility you worked so hard to establish in your market.

I'd like to share one of my favorite techniques with you to help you make all of this happen.

This strategy will show you how to take one piece of content that's very easy for you to create and then distribute it in multiple ways, for maximum reach and usability.

Here is how I do content…

First I film a video blog that goes out virtually every Saturday, trying to keep it around ten minutes max, knowing that it's very difficult to hold people's attention for any longer.

That video blog is then distributed in multiple ways. It goes out as:

- a blog post
- a YouTube video
- an iTunes episode
- at least one Facebook post
- 2-3 Tweets

And if I wanted to, I take the transcript and then copy and paste it in parts to create:

- miniature articles
- a LinkedIn article
- Google+ posts
- an infographic, which I could also use as a Pinterest post

That's nine different possible outlets for one piece of content. And if you spent some time brainstorming about it, I'm sure you could come up with even more.

Vertical Repurposing: Taking one meatier piece of content and breaking it down to distribute to other channels For example, take a podcast or a webinar you recorded and break it down into smaller blog posts, articles, social media posts, infographics, etc.

Horizontal Repurposing: Take a piece of content, such as really good blog post, but then republish it on other channels. Your goal is to get more bang for your buck with your content by promoting it on other distribution channels so you can send new traffic to that same piece of content.

Although this may seem like common sense, or a no-brainer, most people don't have a system. Instead of looking at the myriad of ways a single piece of content can serve them, they stress over creating individual posts for every single different medium.

So, here's my challenge for you. For the medium with which you are most comfortable, focus on creating something on a regular basis *just for that vehicle.* Than, take whatever you create and turn it into multiple pieces of content that are distributed in different ways to captivate different attention points.

Then, once you've done that, here the system I use to get it all done...

1. Schedule time

Every 4-6 weeks, I set aside one day to record 3-4 blog videos. I put these days on my calendar well in advance and make it a habit to give them top priority. I find that when I make creating direct-to-camera videos the focus for just *one* day, I am more creative, present, and in the best frame of mind possible to deliver great content. It's an efficient way to get a lot done in a relatively small amount of focused time.

2. Keep a log of topics

Ideas come to me everywhere. Just the other day, I was at a baseball game with my family, and I started thinking about how the synergy of a great team is complemented by the individuality of each player to create results. My brain started coming up with cool metaphors and stories I could tell to relate this concept to content marketing and production... And so, I pulled out a little notebook that I always carry in my purse to jot down my ideas.

This is how I capture blog ideas. I like to write down potential topics, inspirations, and cool experiences in the moment of inspiration, versus all at once during a forced brainstorming session. This helps create more rich and meaningful content. It makes the topic I share feel more personal to me, and as a result, I believe it makes it more thought-provoking and interesting for my audience as well.

And so, I encourage you to get in the habit of writing topic ideas down as the ideas come. Carry a notebook with you, or set up a place on your smart phone to capture ideas on the go. If you create the mindset to start looking for them, topic ideas will come to you everywhere.

It's hard to just stare at a blank computer screen and force inspiration upon yourself, but if you look for it in real life by paying attention to when you are out and about, great ideas will flow naturally. You just need to initiate the practice of turning that part of your mind on, and then to have a way to capture the insights, observations, and themes that come to you.

If you make this a practice, you will quickly be rewarded because when you sit down to create your video blog, webcast, webinar or podcast, you have all of these ideas already in front of you.

Note: Another way to find ideas (and great thing to do in general) is to go to your Facebook page to see what your online community is most interested in. Study the type of questions they ask, what posts they respond to, and they seem to care about most. On top of keeping a topic log, I also do this every few weeks or so to make sure I am in touch with the pulse of my audience.

3. Produce

There is no excuse to not produce content today. With all of the high-quality digital tools available, what used to only be available to an exclusive wealthy few, is now at our fingertips.

When I first started, my production set-up included: me, my husband and an iPhone. As I've grown I've gotten a little bit more fancy and now have a video person who I hire for the day. But ultimately that isn't absolutely necessary. It just saves me a bit of time and energy, and so it's something I know choose to delegate.

However, you don't need (or want) to overcomplicate your content production—especially if you are on a tight budget or are testing out some initial new ideas. Essentially, a smart phone with video capabilities is really all you need to get going.

Don't get me wrong—I still want it to look good. You will probably want to invest in a graphic designer to ensure your print materials look great, or you may want a little bit of professional help with your video edits. Additionally, you may want someone to give you advice on some basic video best practices—such as filming horizontally in landscape versus vertically in portrait format, or not positioning yourself with something in the background that looks like it's growing out of your head. However, none of these are cost prohibitive barriers that should prevent you from getting your stuff out there.

We are lucky to have so many low-cost options in the world today.

4. Publish

There are a lot of apps out there—such as Hootsuite, Buffer, sprinklr, SocialPilot, or Send. These great, easy tools designed to help you simplify your content distribution by making it simple to preschedule and publish everything. So don't over-think this. Simply choose 5-6 vehicles you want to use to pre-program your content and get it up there. Or, hire an intern to do this part for you.

5. Engage

This is the *most important part* of the production process. However, it is the part the many people overlook. To build the kind of relationships that all of your content was intended to stimulate in the first place, you need to spend time responding to comments, answering questions, and participating in the dialogue your content initiates.

This is where the real connection and value lies.

All the work you've done thus far to streamline the entire life cycle of your content is lost is if you don't seize the opportunity to communicate directly with your audience once you have their attention, and they are seeking yours.

All-in-all, there are endless ways to create and share content—so don't let yourself get caught up in over-*doing* this part. If you focus on making it simple, easy, and fun to implement, you'll be able to reap the rewards by enjoying and appreciating your audience's authentic responses.

CHAPTER FIVE: THE BIG TAKE-AWAY

Our job as content marketers is not to invent information, rather it is to find innovative ways to curate, organize, and share information. By creating systems to help you structure and plan your content's circle of life more efficiently, you will have more time to focus your energy and attention where it matters most—engaging with your audience.

 CHAPTER 5: RESOURCES

To set up an effective circle of life for your content, try answering the following questions:

1 What is one new way you can curate your content?

- Share other content as is
- Provide perspective
- Aggregate—collect the best of other people's research
- Provide access—get influencers to contribute
- Distill—create an overview or summary

2 What framework will best support your message?

- Step-by-step
- Categories or Lists
- Principles / Rules / Laws / Habits
- Common Mistakes (do's vs. don'ts)
- Problems / Solutions
- Storylines
- Series of stories and/or case studies
- Q&A segments or categorized questions
- Model-based framework (uses diagrams based on triangles, systems, or funnels to showcase content)
- Circular-based framework (uses organic, network-based diagrams such as mind-maps to showcase content)

3 When is the best time for you to produce content? How many pieces could you create if you set aside an entire day with this as the focus?

4   What type of topic log works for you (i.e., small notebook, moleskin journal, list on your iPhone, etc.)

5   What medium will you record your core message in?

6   What additional mediums will you use to disseminate it?

7   Who (i.e., an intern) or what (i.e., an app) will distribute your content for you?

8   When will you set aside time to actively engage with your audience?

"

It's not information, by itself, that people are paying you for. It's your ability to share your unique perspective, your ability to structure it so they can use it, and your ability to humanize it that matters.

CHAPTER SIX
FILL UP YOUR BUCKET(S)

*"Give me six hours to chop down a tree,
and I will spend the first four sharpening the axe."*
—Abraham Lincoln

There was once an old farmer who owned an apple tree.

But it was not just any apple tree. The apples from this particular tree were perfectly sweet and full of juicy, crisp flavor. And the tree was perfectly balanced and immensely beautiful as well.

Every spring the apple tree would burst into a fragrant, bouquet of bright pink flowers. And every fall it would yield up to a dozen bushels of apples, which the farmer would sell was able to sell for $100 or more.

One day the farmer decided he was too old to take care of the tree and its harvest, and so he decided to sell it. He placed an ad in a wide-reaching newspaper, hoping to find a buyer with whom he could make a reasonable sale. The ad simply stated: "For sale, apple tree—best fair offer."

The Art of IMPACT

A logger from a neighboring town was the first to answer the ad. He offered to pay $50 for the tree. "That's how much I could make if I cut it down and sold if for firewood," the logger explained.

"You are foolish," the farmer complained. "You only see the tree for its primal value. Perhaps, your price would be good for an ash tree or even for an apple tree no longer bearing fruit. But my tree is worth more than $50. No thank you."

A grocer was next. She offered to pay $100 for the tree. "I plan to harvest and sell this year's crop," she said.

The farmer was somewhat receptive to this offer, but still did not feel that this offer was a fair trade. "You are not quite so foolish as my first buyer. You see this tree has more value as a producer of apples than as a source of firewood. But $100 is not the right price. What of next year's crop? And the many crops after? Your price will not do," he said.

A content marketer then answered the ad. He offered to pay $2,500 for the apple tree.

Upon hearing this offer, the old man raised his eyebrows and then thought about it for a moment before replying with hesitation, "This tree will only produce apples for another 10 years, my friend. In that amount of time, considering inflation, the most you could possibly make from this tree is closer to $1,000. I cannot, in good conscience, take your money. It would not be a fair trade."

But the content marketer did not waver. "Actually, I can make much more from your tree than $1,000," he countered.

"You see—your tree offers much more than just the fruit it bears. It's of such high quality and its branches are so beautiful, I would actually like to invest in harvesting this tree. My plan is to plant its seeds, to nurture them, and to thereby profit from this tree for much longer than just 10 years. Please accept my offer—you can do so in good conscience, as I will be able to profit exponentially on this tree over time."

Considering this thoughtful explanation, the farmer's face broke into a wide grin. "It's a deal," he said.

And they shook hands.

Content marketing employs a special kind of business strategy. Beyond just securing one sale for a single transaction, we look for and appreciate longevity in relationships. By planting seeds, nurturing prospects, and giving relationships time to grow, we afford ourselves the possibility of exponential results and therefore, a much larger payback down the road.

However, in doing so—we must still remember the story of Joshua Bell's flop subway performance. We have to plant the seeds in the *right* places, at the *right* time for them to grow... In other words, you need to get really good at content distribution.

Much like many other parts of the content development process, many content marketers make distribution much more complicated than it needs to be. They spend so much time and energy coming up with big campaign and lead-generation strategies, that they don't really execute any of their distribution efforts effectively.

And then, in a moment of frustration, they throw their hands up in the air and give up on the *entire* process.

Don't let this be you.

The key to content distribution is this—*it only takes a couple of well-executed ideas* to make a big difference in terms of your results.

If your look at any successful business, especially small to mid-sized companies, they generally only have 2-3 well-oiled machines in terms of building leads. They're not out there trying to be everything to everyone and to crack every single lead channel. Instead, they find the couple that work for them, and then they do use those techniques over, and over, and over again.

And so, as you build your content distribution plan, remember— your goal is not to *do everything*, it's to figure out the handful of strategies that work best for you and your business... and then to execute those as seamlessly as possible.

Here's the approach that works for me...

1. KNOW YOUR OUTCOME.

As with everything I build and create, I start by looking at the big picture first in order to create a clear target. I always start with the end in sight by defining a strong outcome. That way I'll know exactly what I am really working to accomplish.

For some, the outcome of content distribution may seem obvious— get more leads to create more sales.

However, because content marketing is a *process* used to build relationships with a buying audience, you will actually want each piece of content in your marketing plan to have a more specialized outcome that drives more specific results.

The greatest mistake is to anticipate the outcome of the engagement; you ought not to be thinking of whether it ends in victory or defeat. Let nature take it's course, and your tools will strike at the right moment.

—*Bruce Lee*

Based on my experience, there are six different possible marketing outcomes you may be seeking any single piece of content.

6 GOALS OF CONTENT

1 Engage with new audiences
2 Build trust and rapport with audience to deepen your connection
3 Drive (the right) leads to your marketing
4 Convert to leads
5 Convert to sales
6 Create customer loyalty and retention

For each distribution-ready piece of content you create, you will want to ask yourself: Which of these six things do I ultimately want this content to deliver?

As an example, if your outcome is to engage with new audiences, you will probably want to think about disseminating your content in a way similar to that of your signature talk. You'll want to focus on using a medium that supports you telling your core story in an especially relatable and personable way.

Or, if your outcome is to create customer loyalty and retention, you'll want to distribute it to clients in way that prevents *everyone* on your list from seeing it. In order to succeed in making your VIPs and most loyal customers feel special, they must be the only ones who can see the offer.

2. START A RELATIONSHIP.

For me, the next step is to think about the people on my distribution list. And then to consider the type of relationship I've established with each part of my list so far.

For marketers, there are ultimately two types of relationships:

2 TYPES OF MARKETING RELATIONSHIPS

1 Those you buy 📦

2 Those you earn ❤️

1. Those you buy

Buying traffic online *can* be a good thing. In doing so, you'll more than likely get more people in. However, the tradeoff is that fewer of them will likely convert.

I think that there can be a lot of benefits to paying for your leads, and that you should absolutely do this if it's right for your business. You just need to understand that paid traffic will require a little bit more finesse in your approach and take more energy to convert.

2. Those you earn

Earned relationships are typically the result of referrals, public relations efforts, social media, and strategic positioning in your field.

It can take more time to build this type of list, but the leads you generate from these sources are much more likely to be the *right* leads for your business. Therefore, when you send out a piece of marketing to them, you know it is reaching a much "warmer" and more receptive audience.

Again, I'm not necessarily saying that one type of relationship is undeniably better than the other; I'm simply making the point that you want to know what type of audience you're working with before you start sending out your content.

3. FILL UP YOUR BUCKETS.

As my friend and fellow marketer, Andy Jenkins, says, "If we're not in front of the cameras, we're not making money."

And so, the next step, metaphorically speaking, is to choose the right medium(s) for you and to "get in front of the cameras" by getting your stuff out there!

There are three basic types of media.

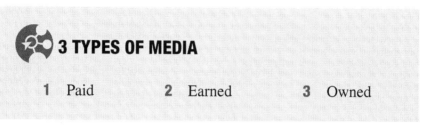

3 TYPES OF MEDIA

1 Paid   2 Earned   3 Owned

Again, the point is not to attempt specializing in each of these potential outlets all at one time. The key is to get one form of traffic working really well, and *then* to extend your reach using additional opportunities.

1. Paid Media

This includes outlets such as:

- ad networks, such as PPC, Outbrain, Taboola, Nativo, or Sharethrough

- paid ads on Facebook, Google, or other channels

- TV, radio and print ads

- Joint Venture partners and affiliates

- pay-per-click

- native advertising, meaning a dynamic piece of marketing, such as an "advertorial" that appears on an informational website or news site and resembles the look and feel of the other pieces of raw data shared there.

Paid content distribution is exactly what the name implies: you're paying to put your content in front of a larger (or new) group of qualified customers. It's advertising you pay for to drive traffic to your owned media.

2. Earned Media

Earned media includes things like:

- traditional media mentions, interviews, articles
- review sites
- word of mouth, referrals

This is important an important outlet because it gives you access to such a large volume of people. (Over 1.55 billion people in the world are currently active users on Facebook, and this number continues to steadily increase every quarter.)

That said, there is one final type of media that is your ultimate goal...

3. Owned Media

Owned media is where you want everyone who reads your stuff to eventually end up. It includes things like:

- your website
- your blog
- your social channels and groups
- your email marketing list
- your direct-mail marketing list

This type of media is powerful and important because it's the only one *you own*. It's the only outlet where you make all the rules, and therefore where you will be able to continue to connect with your audience in the way that most benefits *you*.

I recently asked Robert Rose, Chief Content Strategist at Content Marketing Institute and a friend of mine, "What's the biggest advice you can give me about social media?"

And this is what he told me: "Understand that you don't own it. It's a 'pay to play' set of platforms and they are going to change the rules. And they *will* change the rules. And they will change the rules *at any moment*. The biggest piece of advice I can give you is to get people to you, so you own the relationship."

And so this is what I recommend to you, as well.

As a recap—start by choosing only a few distribution strategies— maybe one paid outlet and one earned outlet. Then, work on mastering those before you add more to your plate. Meanwhile, for every piece of content you distribute, be mindful about how you can ultimately drive your leads back to the media you own, where you will be able to build a much deeper and more personal relationships.

4. GO FOR THE MARATHON, NOT THE SPRINT.

When I first started, I found myself focused on adding a *ton* of value in the front end of my presentations and materials... and then would wrap up at the end by asking my audience to make a purchase using this big, awkward close.

And I hated it.

It didn't work for me personally, and it didn't work for my audience either, as I was not getting the type of results I desired.

I have since learned that it's much more effective, comfortable, and natural to ask for a buy using less dramatic and more personal methods. I now have relationships with people who know that what I have to offer really works. So the "ask" is easy.

That's the innate beauty of content marketing—with every piece of communication, you are organically and honestly enticing prospects to transition into paying customers.

So rather than focusing on one big pitch, I encourage you to concentrate on simply being *consistent.* Go for the marathon instead of the sprint. Ultimately, this approach will make the sales process about a billion times easier.

5. START SMALL AND TEST.

No matter how great your content, the odds are pretty good that you will still have your share of flops.

From time to time, we all have crickets. It's certainly happened to me.

And as a result, I know first-hand how maddening and frustrating it can be to go through a content fail. However, the pain is lessoned greatly if you don't have absolutely everything on the line.

For this reason, I recommend starting small and testing before diving "all in" for every type of new distribution you try.

Then, you will be able to take step back, make needed shifts, and to test again… until you see *real results.*

This is how even the very best marketers create winning campaigns. You may think of your offer as a one-time ask, but it's more of a trial and error review process. Successful marketers take as much time as they need making the same offer multiple times, and in multiple ways, until they hit the jackpot.

The key is simply to keep trying out new angles, new versions, and new techniques until you find one that *really works.*

CHAPTER SIX: THE BIG TAKE-AWAY

At its core, content marketing uses a long-term approach to build relationships that can lead to exponential results. However, in order to reap the potential rewards, you must actively distribute your content by getting it out there and in front of people where you can ask for sales. As you learn how to master this process, don't try to do everything all at once. Instead, start small, test, and find the 2-3 methods that work best for you.

CHAPTER 6: RESOURCES

Here are 5 unique tools you can try out to test for results with your content distribution efforts:

1 OnePress Social Locker—a WordPress plug-in that lets you pre-select and lock a portion of content that readers can click to share on social media

2 Wisestamp—helps you create a custom email signature

3 Goodbits—an email newsletter you can easily drag and drop to customize with your own links and content

4 Boomerang—a feature on Gmail that enables you to schedule emails and automate follow-ups

5 HARO (Help a Reporter)—connects you to journalists looking for new story leads

“

*The greatest good you can do for another is not just
to share your riches, but to reveal to him his own.*

—*Benjamin Disraeli*

PART TWO
TOP 7 CONTENT
MARKETING MISTAKES

NOTE: The following pages contain wisdom abundantly earned through personal experience. Please read carefully and learn from my mistakes!

THE TOP 7 CONTENT MARKETING MISTAKES

Mistake 1: When You Overteach, You Overwhelm

Mistake 2: Structure Before Story

Mistake 3: Promotion Over Production

Mistake 4: You Can't Hide Behind a Computer

Mistake 5: You Are Never Not Marketing

Mistake 6: Great Content Doesn't Mean Great Delivery

Mistake 7: Stop Yelling At Your Cat

CHAPTER SEVEN
MISTAKE 1: WHEN YOU OVERTEACH, YOU OVERWHELM

"Less is more."
—Robert Browning

Point 1—okay, makes sense.

Point 2—I'm with you.

Point 3—nice.

Point 4—interesting… I might remember that later.

Point 5—wait, what were the first two points again? I already forgot!

Point 6—I really hope that my subconscious is absorbing all of this and that it will come back to me when I need it…

Point 7—I wonder how many rooms are in this place? If everyone in this entire event is staying here, and everyone paid the same rate as I did, wow—the hotel is making some great money.

Point 8—did I remember to feed my dog this morning?

Point 9—focus brain, focus… I really want to learn this.

Point 10—I hope we will get a handout that summarizes all of this…

This is the brain on overwhelm.

And it's not pretty.

A mind on overwhelm cannot take in more data… even when it really, *really* wants to. And although each of us have a different limit in terms of how much we can take in before our mind gets lost, starts to wonder, and finally gives up. There is only so much *any* focused mind can take, especially if we are asking ourselves to actually do something with the information being provided.

And for most people, that limit is reached fairly quickly. In fact, for the average human brain, it only takes about three big ideas before the brain begins to feel overloaded and starts to shut down.

Overwhelm may also lead to people feeling unconfident about their ability to comprehend and apply your message… which is exactly the opposite of what you want.

There is a science behind this process.

Here's what happens when you lead people into an information-overload...

First, their brains don't know what data to process first, so the neurons end up trying to multi-task.

Then, when the brain tries to process the multiple ideas all at the same time, a phenomena known as an "attentional blink" occurs. This occurs every time a second stimulus is introduced while the brain is still processing the first. This "blink" is a cognitive gap where the mind actually completely fails to register *any* new sensory information for around 50-150 milliseconds.

By overwhelming your audience, you essentially risk losing their brains for an entire half a second. Every time you do it.

It gets worse.

Because the brain is not able to handle two stimuli simultaneously, a person attempting to understand more than one concept at a time will temporarily suffer from what it is known as a "psychological refractory period," or PRP. This condition directly impairs a person's ability to make even simple decisions... which means they will not be able to figure out how to act on or even engage in the rest of the information you shared, even the ideas that they previously understood... before you high-jacked their brains.

So, if providing tons of information does not serve our audience, why do we it?

As far as I can tell, there are two main reasons why, as content producers, we tend to err on over-delivery:

1. We have a genuine desire to give.

I believe this is the primary reason we tend to overload our content. We have the best intentions in mind and truly just want our clients to succeed. So we feel compelled to give them absolutely everything we can think of to ensure results.

But by being so caught up in sharing all this value, we disconnect with the audience's current state and don't realize they are no longer able to actively receive the gifts we're sharing.

The second reason for over-delivering is a bit more complex…

2. We are afraid that our content is not "enough."

Sometimes we put out a *ton* of data, and words, and graphics, and statistics… because we're afraid we won't succeed otherwise. We don't trust that our knowledge is strong enough, that we have enough credentials, or that our delivery style is professional enough for people to want it… and so we try to compensate by simply adding in more *stuff*.

Our effort is still genuine—we just want to make sure the value is there to justify the attention we are asking for… but unfortunately, this plan almost always backfires by turning people off before our content even has a chance to shine.

So, here's the bottom line—no matter what type of content you are creating—whether it is a sales letter, a blog, or a presentation, be sure to give your audience space to process what you're sharing… and don't share too much!

Instead, encourage concentration and focus with your content, and set your audience up to win by creating a straightforward path for them.

Here are a few essential content best practices you can use to help people take in your materials more readily:

1. PROVIDE PRACTICAL TOOLS AND STRATEGIES.

When your audience is forced to figure out what to *do* with the information you share, you are indirectly giving them yet another something to think about. In contrast, when you give them the practical next steps that coincide with your message right away, it frees up the brain space they would use to try to figure this out on their own, so they can relax and go back to concentrating on your message instead.

2. MIND-READ THEIR EMOTIONAL STATE AND PROVIDE ENCOURAGEMENT.

When people feel like they are "getting something," they will stay connected and keep pushing their brains to keep up. However, the opposite is true when people start to feel like they don't understand or aren't following.

To help manage the emotional roller-coaster associated with a learning curve, you first have to know its there. Know this and remind yourself of it regularly. Simply being more aware of your client's potential struggle will help keep you in check.

Then, pay attention to where people tend to ask a lot of questions, or where you get blank stares during a presentation. Then, remember to provide encouragement and support, especially in those key places.

The key is to use their excitement to keep them motivated, while building confidence and clarity to help them make real progress. When people feel like they are getting something, they will stay on the path.

3. MAKE SURE YOUR CONTENT IS READABLE AND EASY TO FOLLOW.

To keep your audience on track and out of overwhelm, here are some of my best organization tips.

- Keep your content to one thought or idea per "chunk" of information.

- Use relatable language and simple words. (At readability-score.com, you can paste your copy into a window, and it will give you a score for both reading ease and grade level.)

- Be precise. Usually this requires using fewer words to get your point across, which requires more specificity and thought. When we are not clear about something ourselves, we tend to over-explain.

- Break it down to the ridiculous. Tell your audience the very first thing they can do to make progress. Make sure they get good at that. And then, move on.

- Give examples of how what you're sharing has successfully been applied in the real world. Examples help people get emotionally attached to why what you're sharing is important, and that helps them remember it.

And, the next time you feel yourself trying to pack all your best tips all into one little piece of content, rein yourself back in! Finally, remember, less is more.

CHAPTER SEVEN: THE BIG TAKE-AWAY

Although well intentioned, too much content is a turn-off for audiences. Work to keep your copy short, sweet, and to the point.

CHAPTER EIGHT
MISTAKE 2: STRUCTURE BEFORE STORY

"The universe is built on a plan the profound symmetry of which is somehow present in the inner structure of our intellect."
—Paul Valery

Close your eyes for just a moment and imagine your favorite song. Take a moment to really get it in your head... so that you actually feel the timing, the rhythm, and the cadence.

You can even close this book for a moment to actually play it helps, and if you have a musical device nearby...

I am assuming you are now back with me.

Now, close your eyes one more time and imagine hearing all the right notes played, but all over the place, out of rhythm, and without any structure. What would that feel like?

Hearing even your favorite song like this would likely be unpleasant... and even stressful for most people.

And there is a reason for this disconnect.

All music is based on mathematics. The frequency created by a certain set of sounds can actually be calculated and computed. And without a balanced "equation," it creates what is known in musical terms as "discord," or the lack of harmony between notes and sounds.

My mom was a music teacher, and she used to demonstrate the peculiarity of this sensation with the song "Happy Birthday" to show me how it worked. Listening to the song played without rhythm, but using the correct notes is equal parts fascinating and painful to hear. It actually creates a sense of anxiety because the song is all over the place and you can't really tell what's coming next.

Even more interesting, however, is this—when my mom would play "Happy Birthday" with a solid structure, but using all the *wrong* notes, it was much more tolerable. In fact, it was even sort of entertaining.

Why is this?

Structure is the container our brains put ideas and concepts in to make them make sense. Like super-powered, computer processors, we look for recognizable patterns in order to calculate and understand the world around us.

In fact, if we don't have that structure or cannot recognize it, our mind will get stuck, wrapped up, or even totally consumed by its inability to figure out what is going on. It's sort of like trying to pack up and move the contents of entire house without having a box to put stuff in.

Our brains need containers to pack in ideas and take them with us.

This is especially important to understand when you weave stories into your content. Although stories are a powerful way to stimulate emotion and build personal rapport, the message will get completely lost if there is no structure there.

A story without structure can leave an audience feeling as though they have walked into a movie about 20 minutes late. Parts of it can feel sort of entertaining, but for the most part, you feel compelled to keep nudging the person next to you so that you can catch up on the plot.

"So, who is that guy?"

"He's the best friend of the guy who is the main character."

"Is he in a relationship with that girl?"

"No that's his sister."

"Why are they driving so fast in the middle of the woods?"

"Someone is chasing them."

"Who? Why?!"

You get the idea.

Unless you have a great friend sitting next to you, who is capable of covertly whispering just the right amount of information into your ear to get you caught up on what you missed, it can be pretty exhausting to try to figure out the plot-line all on your own.

A story without structure feels the same way.

And this is a mistake I see content marketers make a lot.

In contrast, you can find a great example of well-structured content by watching educational children's programs. There have been a decent number of studies performed on how kids learn, and based on that data, children's programs are intentionally set up with several clear, constant, and predictable elements.

Blue's Clues and *Sesame Street* are good examples.

In *Blue's Clues*, the adorable puppy, Blue, *always* interacts with a human character to solve a mystery. She *always* puts her paw prints on three clues. At some point, she *always* looks at the camera and asks for help from viewers. And the human *always* wears a colorful striped sweater. The show makes kids feel like they are detectives, as they often get actively involved in the plot. It's even pretty addictive for adults because you kind of get drawn in and want to know what Blue will end up solving.

Sesame Street actually has almost too many structural anchors associated to review the show in its entirety, at least within the confines of this book. However, one of my favorite characters is a good example of one the many ways the show's producers use structure to build certainty. Oscar the Grouch is *always* annoyed when a visitor knocks on his trashcan, because such a disruption *always* interrupts him from a nap or some "important" trash-related task. And most importantly, he is *always* grouchy… and he is *always* trying to pass that feeling on to everyone else.

Producers know that kids learn best when they can anticipate the structure behind each episode. Having certainty about what's coming builds their confidence and therefore makes them more open-minded about the learning opportunities presented.

The same is true for adult learners.

When content is presented with a clear structure, it allows us to anticipate what's coming and thereby helps us proactively construct a framework to put it in.

Here are a few examples of "adult" content created with great structure:

- *The 5-Minute Debt Solution: Get Out Fast and Stay Out Forever* by my husband, Chris Hendrickson.

  Although I am a little biased, I know how well this book works. And I know it is at least partly because it takes a seemingly complex topic and breaks it down into three really solid steps: (1) Get out of debt fast, (2) Stay out of debt forever, and (3) Invest in your long-term dreams.

- The United States Constitution.

  This document is also broken down into three clear parts: (1) The Preamble, (2) the Articles, and (3) the Amendments.

  This document would not have worked to serve our country for the past two centuries if there wasn't an established core structure with clearly defined rules around that structure. And because people understand that structure, they can contribute and use the information as guiding communal principles.

- *The Wizard of Oz,* by L. Frank Baum (film produced by Metro-Goldwyn-Mayer)

  I love this one. The storyline of this classic movie actually has a clear structure that takes viewers full circle. We start in Kansas, go to Munchkin Land, get on the Yellow Brick Road, go to Emerald City, and then go back to Kansas. And there is a specific color that represents each location, starting with black and white in Kansas at the start of the movie and full color by the return back home.

The movie's theme, "There's no place like home," reinforces the entire journey. Although this is an emotional story, part of what makes us appreciate it is that the structure behind the story makes it so easy to follow and remember.

So, don't skimp on structure. It is the hidden formula behind all great works. Here are some tips to help…

1. Provide an overview.

Give people a clear overview explaining what you are going to share. Then, stay true to that framework. And at the end, recap your message. In other words: Tell them what you will tell them. Tell them. Tell them what you told them.

2. Create steps.

Numbers are great because they let readers know exactly where they are in a process. Smaller numbers work best for most "how-to" information, such as "5 Easy Steps to Optimize Your Marketing Funnel," or "3 Simple Rules in Life." However, larger lists can be a creative way to showcase lists, such as "100 Best Marketing Tips," "Top 50 Quotes from Small Business Owners."

3. Base it on logic.

Whether your content is organized sequentially, by category, by priority, or in some other way, it all works. They type of organization you use doesn't really matter; it's the logic *behind* the organization that does. As long as readers can understand the structure you create, they will be able to follow and remember the content you share.

4. Create a trajectory.

Make sure your content leads people to someplace better than where they were before they read, watched, or listened to it. Move them forward in some way towards the type of excellence they aspire to achieve.

5. Provide your information in chunks.

Break the information down into pieces and then provide great titles people will remember for each component. If you can accomplish making it both simple and catchy all at the same time, the data will require less effort for people to remember and apply.

6. Incorporate a visual diagram or metaphor.

Visual aids help people relate to and understand where they are in the process. It gives them a picture they can hold in their mind to keep track of both how far they have come and where they are going.

Overall, taking the time to incorporate elements such as these and to plan our your content's structure sets your audience up to win. And their win is your success.

 **CHAPTER EIGHT: THE BIG TAKE-AWAY**

By giving your audience a structure to support their learning, they are much more apt to both retain and enjoy the content you share.

"

*The key to a successful learning environment
is structure.*

—Cara Carroll, First Grade Teacher

CHAPTER NINE
MISTAKE 3: PROMOTION OVER PRODUCTION

*"It had long since come to my attention that people
of accomplishment rarely sat back and let things happen
to them. They went out and happened to things."*
—Leonardo da Vinci

Before Peter Lik became a well-known photographer and was featured in his own show "From the Edge with Peter Lik" on the Weather Channel, he was a simply a greeting card salesman who regularly traveled with his camera and made a point to take a lot of photographs. Eventually Lik was able to turn his photographs into a successful postcard business, and soon afterwards, he opened up his first gallery in his hometown—Queensland, Australia.

Then, just 10 years after his humble beginning, Lik astonished the professional art community and made world headlines when he sold one of his photographs for $6.5 million to an anonymous buyer—the most ever paid for a single photographic print.

Now known as the world's most expensive photograph, the image, entitled, "Phantom," is a well-balanced and beautiful print. It captures a mysterious human-shaped swirl of dust dancing in a natural spotlight formed within Arizona's Antelope Canyon.

However, based on the standards of most art collectors, the photograph is woefully unworthy of such a high price.

"I've never even heard of him," Martin Parr, a renowned British photographer, said of "Phantom," in an article that ran in England's The Independent.

"It's pretty astonishing. I've looked at his work today and though he's a very good commercial photographer who can take pictures people like, he has no standing whatever in the fine-art world that I belong to."

And the same sentiment is shared for other pricey Lik pieces. (He holds three other spots on the list of 20 most expensive photographs of all time.)

"It's an abomination," Michael Hoppen, a leading British photography gallerist, said.

"I remember when he sold the picture in 2010, my jaw dropped. I thought, who could be persuaded to part with $1 million (pounds) for a piece of that? You could have done it with an iPhone."

So how did Lik do it?

How did he convince people to part with so much money to purchase his arguably somewhat average photographs?

Promotion.

Peter Lik is, and always has been, a genius at promoting his work.

Nearly every photograph he sells is printed as a "limited edition." Making only 995 prints of each image, he usually sells the first print for around $4,000. Then, the price continually increases as the edition sells out. For example, after 40 percent of the prints have been sold, the price may rise by $500, after 90 percent of the prints have been sold, the price may rise by $1,300, and so on.

Lik also sells 45 "artist's proofs" of every photograph. All of the images are identical. However, Lik has created a demand for artist's proofs because he deems them more prestigious, and is therefore able to command as much as $10,000 as a starting price for these esteemed prints.

In a 2015 article in The New York Times, author David Segal explains how Lik's prices can quickly accelerate even more from there:

"When 95 percent of an image has sold it becomes 'Premium Peter Lik' and the price jumps to $17,500. At 98 percent, it's 'Second Level Premium Peter Lik' and leaps to $35,000. And when the image gets down to its last handful, the prices can go as high as $200,000 or more. When all copies of a photograph are sold, it can gross the company more than $7 million. The message is that the sooner you buy, the less you will pay. So buy now."

Beyond crafting a brilliant sales strategy, Lik is also not shy about publicizing his success and using that as momentum to further his brand recognition. After the record-breaking sale of "Phantom," he was fast to hire a PR firm to help him publicize the story, and as a result, was featured in headlines in hundreds of publications around the world as the artist behind "the world's most expensive photograph."

Every part of Lik's sales process is maximized and evaluated. Gallery sales reps are called "art representatives," and each one is required to attend a four-day sales training course prior to working the gallery floor. Each showroom is put together in a way that invites a relaxed vibe—it celebrates the photographs in a way that sells a certain *lifestyle* or feeling as people linger to review the pieces.

In fact, Lik is such a master of promotion, I could spend another several pages detailing the many additional ways he smartly and creatively drives sales.

And so whether you are a fan of Peter Lik's photographs or not, the moral to this story is pretty clear—it's not necessarily the art that matters; it's the marketing.

In fact, there is absolutely zero correlation between great content and the number of people who end up seeing and appreciating it. When all is said and done, popularity comes down to who has done a better job promoting their work.

As content creators, this is an important lesson.

It is really easy for us to get caught up in our efforts to perfect our work. Typically, content creators *enjoy* producing new materials. We get sort of "geeked out" by information, stories, and new ways of presenting data. That's what makes us good as what we do.

However, as much as we can easily get carried away with production, we must train ourselves to spend more time on promotion if we want to be able to actually profit from all of our hard work.

This requires a shift in mindset.

As a rule of thumb, for the amount of time you spend creating a piece of content, I recommend you spend about five times that amount promoting it.

This may seem like a tall order, especially when you consider that most content creators currently engage in exactly the opposite distribution of their time—spending four to five times more hours every day on production instead of promotion.

But the pay-back is worth it.

The concept is cleanly aligned with a well-known theory known as "Pareto's Law." Created by economist-sociologist, Vilfredo Pareto, who lived from 1848-1923, Pareto's Law has become more commonly referred to in the past decade as, "The 80/20 Principle."

The gist of the theory can be summarized pretty simply: 80 percent of the output from any one thing usually stems from 20 percent of the input.

Applying this principle to content marketing, your best results will happen when you spend:

- 80 percent of your time on promotion, and

- 20 percent of your on production.

For me, transitioning to this type of mindset has paid off in ways I didn't expect. I can see now that when I used to focus on just continually putting out great content, my approach was pretty linear. I would create something, put it out there, and then move onto the next piece.

Shifting my focus has made my work-flow much more dynamic and interesting. The content I create is now more of an interactive experience with my audience.

I will create something. Then, entice people by engaging with them directly. Based on their feedback, I may then refine that piece of content before I put it out there. Then, after testing and finding out how the content actually lands with my audience, I may go back and refine it again so that I can deliver it in a totally different place or maybe just with a different frame to the same audience.

Using this type of mindset, every piece of content live a much more dynamic life before it is either considered "complete" or temporarily retired.

The key to making this type of shift work for you is to start making the maximization of your promotion over production a *habit*.

You have to hold yourself accountable and really think about where you are spending your time, *every day* to make the change.

I'm not saying this is easy, but I can say it will be worth it.

Easy is staying in our comfort zone... Easy (or at least "easier") is simply focusing on creating content, one piece at a time. Easy is doing what we have always done... and getting the same results.

I want more for you. And I know you have it in you.

Get strong. And stretch yourself with this concept to work towards splitting your time in this manner. The pay-offs will be worth it.

CHAPTER NINE: THE BIG TAKE-AWAY

However much you enjoy producing new master works of genius content, the time you spend masterfully promoting your work is what will actually pay you down the road.

CHAPTER TEN
MISTAKE 4: YOU CAN'T HIDE BEHIND A COMPUTER

"Well done is better than well said."
—Benjamin Franklin

A client once asked me very earnestly,

"You know all that engagement stuff? Can I just outsource that?"

Upon hearing this question, I had to smile.

No matter how much you love just sitting behind your computer and creating and promoting great content, you cannot just hire someone to do "that engagement part" for you.

You can't outsource a relationship.

By nature of its definition, a relationship requires two or more people to both contribute to and benefit from an exchange. It's a personal and mutually appreciated sharing of energy and value. And you can only create a genuine connection if there are two invested parts.

Trying to out-source interaction with your clients is sort of like saying to your spouse, "I'll do the bed, make the dinner, and we can split up watching the kids, but let's hire someone else to manage our time together."

Relationships are *personal*, and therefore they require a personal approach.

Interacting with your clients is about creating a one-on-one connection that let's them know you really care about them, their successes, and their challenges. It's an opportunity to reinforce their progress, to encourage their wins, and to incentive them to even more deeply engage the products and services you offer.

And this level of connection isn't something you can hire someone else to create.

Nonetheless, I am amazed by how many disengaged business owners have come to me over the years asking me to help them increase their profitability, and who don't even realize their lack of connection with their audience is a big deterrent. Nor, do they even have any idea how to simply interact with their clients.

If you think this might describe how you interact with audience, I have news for you—your business is "out there" with customers, not "in here" inside your office.

The most successful people in content marketing actually get out there and meet new people. They go to events, they network, they develop relationships with other thought leaders and influencers in their field, and they spend time really getting to know their clients.

Engagement is a process, not a one-time task or objective you can delegate.

In fact, I believe our lack of interest in getting to know people is one of the negative consequences of our digital world. Ironically, it seems that since we communicate with nearly anywhere and at any time, we have become somewhat numb to the value of genuinely responding to people and nurturing relationships.

This will date me. I remember when I was a kid, we had one of those old rotary phones in our house—the kind with the big dial and super long, spiral cord. If you were both in the second half of the 21st century, you may be familiar with these, or at least have seen them at your grandparents' house.

For several years growing up, the big, rotary dial phone was the only phone in the house, and it was the only way to reach any one of my family members. There was no such thing as cell phones, or email, or certainly not online social media apps at the time. So whenever the phone rang, it was sort of exciting. The person calling was making an effort to reach out to someone in my family, and so that person was important to us.

We would pause a movie so that someone could get up and answer the phone, or take a break from whatever else was going on to pick up the phone and then take the time to genuinely connect with the person on the either end of the phone.

Our world has changed a lot since then, but when I respond to people on social media, I try to remember the quality of the types of conversations I had on that big old rotary phone. Metaphorically speaking, I pretend that my "phone" rings anytime any of the following occurs on social media.

5 WAYS YOUR PHONE "RINGS" ON SOCIAL MEDIA

1 When someone comments on your post

2 When someone likes or shares a piece of content

3 When someone makes inquires (emails support or calls your business)

4 When someone mentions you in another post, tweet, or share

5 When someone tags you in a post or photo

This might seem like a lot to manage.

To bring engagement to the forefront and make it a business priority, it helps to create a plan. You don't want to take this too far and become a martyr for your clients either, by spending all your time instantly responding to social media queries or comments.

Ultimately, you will need to make your own decisions about what you what you can effectively outsource, but as long as you take responsibility and feel as though you *own* the relationship, there are interactions that you can train others to handle for you.

So, what does it make sense to do yourself, and what types of communication *can* you successfully outsource to other people?

For me, the two areas that I usually outsource are:

1. Customer service

I can train people to be somewhat of a host or traffic guide when clients have process-related questions about my business. The difference for me is that the types of questions that come up in this department are usually related to the logistical and technical aspects of my business, not the actual application and use of content. And frankly, some of the people I have hired can provide more certainty and direction related to these areas than I can.

2. Sales

Especially as your business starts to grow, it will be hard for any one person to manage sales. From even just a mathematical perspective, the odds of landing more sales will be better if you have more people reaching out and contacting people. For me, having a person or team of people constantly focused on filling up my pipeline so that I always have new prospects at various stages in my marketing funnel is a very helpful, smart way to outsource.

In contrast, there are certain communications that I never outsource.

They are:

1. Answering content questions

When someone is engaged and interested in a piece of content that I've created and asks me a question about it, I feel it is essential to take the time to thoroughly answer and respond. I value this type of interaction as a crucial opportunity to create a lasting dialogue with my audience.

Plus, after putting so much time into thinking about and anticipating my clients' needs, when someone brings a real query or concern to the table, it helps me stay more in touch with who my clients really are and what they really need. Being on the "front-line" is a way to stay relevant. And as I hope that I've emphasized throughout this book, that is an extraordinarily significant piece of intel when working to create effective content marketing that really works.

If I am out-of-town, recording, or otherwise unavailable, I will have someone cover communications online for me. However, for anything that is in my "voice," I make sure that I see and approve it before it goes out.

2. Social media

This one may surprise you. I am certainly asked about it a lot.

And I have struggled with it, as well. When I first started, this seemed like an obvious area to outsource.

But as hard as I tried, I could not find anyone who could do this for me. It can be a pretty constant and tedious communication platform to stay on top of, but it's highly personal as well. And as a result, when I had other people do it for me, it just didn't work. To compete with all the other many content platforms out there, this was a place where personalization really made a big difference for me.

After going back and forth about how to handle this for a while, I finally asked a few other busy thought leaders how they handled social media and what they recommended. Of the people I asked, all humbly admitted that they had come to the same conclusion as me.

And at this point, if you come and visit my Facebook or Twitter pages, you will know that you are communicating directly with me, as I now write my own posts.

3. Events

While onsite at events, I *always* take the time to connect with participants one-on-one. This type of interaction is a rare opportunity to genuinely create a human bond, and I don't take that type of communication lightly.

By making these occurrences more personal, it makes it easier for me to connect in a meaningful way. And as a result, I feel inspired to give each communication the honor and respect that it deserves.

This has helped my business a ton.

And it can do for the same for you.

So get out there… and start getting to know the people surrounding your business! It's a big world out there beyond your computer.

CHAPTER TEN: THE BIG TAKE-AWAY

Engagement isn't some marketing term that you can check off a "to-do" list. Engagement requires a genuine emotional connection. And when you are building content-marketing-based relationships by putting your content online, that's where you want to spend a decent portion of your time.

"

Content is King but engagement is Queen, and the lady rules the house!

—Mari Smith

CHAPTER ELEVEN
MISTAKE 5: YOU ARE NEVER NOT MARKETING

*"The greatest ability in business is to get along with others
and to influence their actions."*
—John Hancock

When I first started working for Tony Robbins at his company, Robbins Research International, people would often come to me in the Creative Department and ask marketing-related questions.

And each time I received an annoying query of this nature, I would defensively point in the opposite direction and calmly explain, "I'm not marketing. It's on the other side of the building."

The truth is I was totally intimidated by even the idea of marketing. It seemed so starkly analytic, numbers-driven, black and white, and simply cold. I wasn't into any of that. I had been inspired to work Tony's company because I wanted to change people's lives and inspire them to do great things, not manipulate them into spending money.

What I didn't realize at the time was that these two objectives were completely intertwined. Both inspiring people to change their lives and inspiring them to spend money on our events and services required the ability to strategically influence our clients to act in their own best interest.

In fact, influence is the core component of absolutely every piece of quality content written. None of it matters very much if you don't have the ability to convince your audience to pay attention to you in the first place, or if you are unable to persuade them at every step of their journey to continue engaging with your content.

As content marketers, we need to be able to motivate an audience to even want to open up our blog, and then we have to be able to get them to read it, to engage with, to be excited about it… and to *want* to share it. Somehow we have to be able to get inside the heads of our clients and prospects, to become a part of their inner dialogue, and to encourage them to *do something*.

In fact, a piece of content without a clear objective is a mess of purposeless words and phrases. Without influence, the content goes absolutely nowhere and remains hopelessly inactive and meaningless.

For this reason, if we are creating content that is worth reading, watching, or listening to, whether we like the idea or not, we are *always* marketing.

But contrary to my initial misconception, good marketing is not manipulation.

From an ethical standpoint, the key is to be mindful about what you are moving someone to do. Whereas manipulation is the result of pushing someone to do something that only serves *your best interests*, ethically sound marketing inspires someone to do something that services *their best interests*. As a marketer, your goal is always to help people get what *they want*.

And at the end of the day, marketing will always be more effective and yield a higher return than manipulation.

To accomplish this, here are some of the best marketing tips I have learned over the years.

1. Know what is *already important to them.*

A big part receiving permission to get be a part of another person's inner dialogue is to really understand who they are and what they are about. You have to fully step into their shoes, to see the world from their vantage point, and fully understand and respect their perspective.

Only then will you be able to move them to see the action you'd like them to take as something that coincides with the direction in which they are already moving.

2. Remove all judgment.

This is something I learned from my time working with Tony Robbins—you cannot influence someone when you're judging him or her. If you think less of a person because of where he or she is at in life, or if you don't approve of the past decisions that may have created his or her present circumstances, you will not have earned the right to influence any future actions.

Influence is only possible when you come from a place of total and complete unconditional support.

That said, it is important to note that there is a marked difference between pushing someone to reach his or her full capabilities and judging his or her ability to get there. Calling someone out because you see what is possible is not the same as directly (or indirectly) creating even the slightest feeling of shame or disapproval.

3. Don't be afraid to ask for the action.

This advice comes from a TED Talk called, *The Paradox of Choice* by psychologist Barry Schwartz. In short, the key takeaway is this—by popular assumption, if we all have more choices, we will be happier. However, according to Schwartz's research, the opposite is true—the more choices we give people, the *less* happy they actually are. Too many options can actually create stress, confusion, overwhelm, and ultimately analysis paralysis.

So make it clear what you want people to *do* with your content. There is a time and place when it is absolutely appropriately to simply tell your audience what to do.

4. Use social proof.

When people see that other people are getting results that they crave for themselves, they pay attention. So, look for ways to showcase your client's success stories, and ask them for testimonials.

What other people say about you is more powerful than anything you say about yourself.

5. Be 1,000 percent trust-worthy.

Sadly, trust is at an all-time low in our world today. It's a rare commodity, and therefore something that people gravitate toward when found. To build (and maintain) your audience's trust:

- always have their best interest in mind

- be transparent and open about what you are doing

- when you say you will do something, *do it*

6. Listen.

You cannot start telling other people what to do until you stop and listen to the ideas they have first. People need to know that you relate to them and understand the challenges, obstacles, and distractions that may have previously been in their way.

They also need to feel confident that you completely "get" what they want to accomplish and are on the same page in terms of why it matters.

So be willing to be flexible, and make sure your clients know they are being heard by adapting your communication style when necessary.

Lastly, remember to use all of this wisdom ethically and responsibly. These are great tools that can help you be more conscious about how you move and inspire people. But your outcome should always be in your client's best interest.

CHAPTER ELEVEN: THE BIG TAKE-AWAY

In content (and in life), we are always influencing others to respond and connect with us in some way. Although we don't typically think of ourselves this way, we are all marketers. Knowing this, we can make a positive impact in the world by consciously using ethical principles to motivate people to act in their own best interest.

"

Marketing is too important to be left to the marketing department.

—David Packard

Pam Hendrickson

CHAPTER TWELVE
MISTAKE 6: GREAT CONTENT DOESN'T MEAN GREAT DELIVERY

"Nothing endures but change."
—Heraclitus

2000: A man named Reed Hastings approaches Blockbuster Video executives and gives them the opportunity to partner with him in establishing his struggling online video rental site, Netflix. Upon making the offer, Hastings is essentially laughed out of the room.

2004: Blockbuster is at the peak of its prime. The company is worth about $5 billion, and they have about 9,000 stores located worldwide. They notice that the once fledgling Netflix is starting to gain traction with consumers, so they decide to create their own online video subscription service.

2005: Blockbusters starts to see their profits decline.

2007: After going through several different CEOs, each of whom attempt to reverse the company's painful and relentless regression, Blockbuster executives resolve that they should focus solely on their original business model. So, the company drops their online division and invests everything they have left back into their traditional retail stores.

125

2010: Blockbuster Video files for bankruptcy.

2014: All corporate-owned Blockbuster Video retail stores are closed. Netflix, of course, is thriving.

In a single decade, Blockbuster Video managed to go from one of the most successful companies in the United States to completely non-existent.

Why?

Because the company failed to respond to rapid changes in both technology and consumer demand. Rather than adapting their delivery style to the growing interest in more versatile viewing options, Blockbuster chose to stay in their comfort zone.

Even when the company made an attempt to expand into an online distribution platform, they did so without understanding the needs and demands of their web-based audience. Rather than altering their approach to strategically serve a new generation of consumers, the company simply tried to combine what they thought was working for Netflix with a version of their original, trusted business model.

Needless to say, it didn't work.

And as content providers, this is a mistake we cannot afford to make. Just as Blockbuster experienced, the moment we fail to adapt to change is the moment we begin to fail.

This is especially true in a world that seems to come up with new technological mechanisms to support content distribution on a weekly basis.

I used to think that I could just take my content and drop it online to accommodate my digital audience. And, I've often had clients ask me to do the same thing. In fact, just a few weeks ago, someone asked me if I could take his audio program from 1973 and turn it into an online course without adding any additional content to it.

Unfortunately, I had to turn him down, as I have learned that switching content from one delivery vehicle to another is not such a simple thing to do, unless you're willing to invest in some additional delivery tools.

Here's what it would take:

- The entire tone of the presentation would need to shift, meaning we'd need to remove some old references that don't make sense anymore as well as add some framing so there's a modern context to the material.

- We would have to create several new visual elements to support the content by putting the audio to visuals with sound and/or music, by filming some video to augment the audio, and/or investing in some audio editing to augment the sound quality as much as possible.

- We'd have to trim the lessons down into much shorter snippets to accommodate a shorter online attention span, which would likely make it harder to successfully get each point across.

All things considered, it would actually end up being more cost-effective to start from scratch then to edit and transform an old audio program to force it into a totally different medium.

Keeping this in mind, as you work to create content for a variety of possible vehicles out there, I advise you keep two key principles in mind.

1. Match your content to the delivery vehicle.

Some environments are more intimate than others. Others require content that is very succinct and direct.

As an example, it would normal to lean my head on my husband's shoulder while in a movie theater. However, while in a business meeting, that would be a really weird thing to do. The same is true when you deliver your content. Think about how your audience will be taking in the information and then make sure you're giving it to them in a way that's consistent and natural for them.

In other words, you will want to choose the medium that most naturally supports your content and vice versa.

Now, don't be afraid to use content that's from a different time. In fact, some of my favorite client projects have involved taking video, audio or writing from a leader who's passed on, and creating a training program from it. The key is to take the core message and themes—which are evergreen—but the apply the *delivery* to a current platform. By adding visual effects to frame old video, including introductions and voiceovers from modern leaders, and adding some explanation behind why this message is still relevant today, you can turn this type of content into a modern day hit.

2. Adapt your own style to that mechanism.

Because the medium influences the message, you also need to be able to mindfully adapt your style accordingly.

For example, when delivering an online webinar, you need to approach your audience slightly differently then you would if you were teaching to a live crowd on stage in a hotel ballroom.

That said, you don't need to over-think this. For the most part, you can use common sense to dictate how you put together for different types of content platforms. Here are a few examples:

- Mobile devices: Keep it short and sweet. People are usually doing more than one thing at a time while on their phone or tablet, or they in a location that is competing for their attention. As a result, you have to keep content intended for this type of consumption highly visual, easy to follow, direct, and to-the-point.

- Twitter: Share short, clever, and quick snippets.

- White paper: Deliver richly researched content, and present it with a more scholarly tone. Include a bibliography and properly cite all associated research.

- Speaking engagements: Start with a core story and focus on building rapport with the audience. Then, continually read the energy of the audience to maintain that connection throughout your talk.

- Webinars: Keep the core story much shorter, as people online tend to have a much shorter attention span. Include more visuals. Slow way down to give people time to take in the information, knowing that they will likely be doing more one thing as they listen to you.

Keeping your content and delivery styles nimble enough to keep up with the ever-changing forms of technology today isn't necessarily difficult. It first requires an awareness of what is out there and most current.

Then, you simply need to practice thinking about your message from the perspective of a variety of different media platforms. And the more you do it, the easier it will get.

CHAPTER TWELVE: THE BIG TAKE-AWAY

Staying in touch with changing technological and consumer demands is imperative for survival in our quickly evolving world. And in order to shift your content to support a variety of potential mediums, you need to be able to make intelligent adaptations, which requires awareness, flexibility, and practice.

"

Speech is power: speech is to persuade,
to convert, to compel.

—Ralph Waldo Emerson

CHAPTER THIRTEEN
MISTAKE 7: STOP YELLING AT YOUR CAT

"A man who carries a cat by the tail
learns something he can learn in no other way."
—Mark Twain

I have spent more time and energy than I care to admit trying to control what I can't change in both my business and my content.

And in essence, I have learned that the absurdity of doing something so ineffective makes about as much sense as yelling at my cat.

My cat doesn't respond. He can't fix my problem. He cannot change the situation. He cannot even yell back. No matter how I upset I get, he just looks up at me with his typical ambivalent and neutral cat-stare and licks his paws.

He couldn't care any less.

But perhaps this nonchalant response from my cat is actually the best advice I could receive—to simply accept those things beyond my control as they are, and not get so wrapped in the things I cannot change.

Here are few examples of the types of scenarios that (if I let them) could once ruin my day:

- technology not working correctly

- weird comments on my social media pages

- getting "crickets," i.e., no response at all on posts

- sending out a sales message that doesn't convert

- disconcerting world events

Maybe you can relate?

Over time, I have learned that I have a choice in terms of how I respond to these situations. I can either waste my time getting angry about these types of things, or simply accept them the way they are. And move on.

Without fail, the latter always works out to be a better choice.

In my experience, taking these types of things personally is a total waste of time and energy.

I have spent hours getting overly worried about something that is already done and over and the better portion of an entire day obsessively logging back into my Facebook page, hoping for more "likes" and comments.

I have spent entire dinner conversations lamenting to my husband about a "not-so-friendly" comment or complaint, and I have missed out on quality time with my sons because I was too busy in my head, toiling over whether or not my latest content creation was "good enough."

And what was the result of all these efforts? Absolutely nil.

When all was said and done, actions such as these got me absolutely nowhere. This type of behavior is like weighing yourself five times per day, and hoping to see the number change. Or, waiting next to the phone all day for some guy you like to call.

It's pointless.

Your time and energy, like mine, is so valuable—so please learn from my mistakes in this arena.

Focus on what you can influence, not on what you can't control.

Focus on the quality and consistency of what you are putting out there. Focus on finding great stories, on recognizing the efforts of your most outstanding clients, on finding new inspirations, and on feeling grateful for what you already have.

Spend your free time really being fully "there" with your family and friends. Spend your precious head-space coming up with creative new ideas and sharing them. And spend your energy on celebrating what *is* right in the world.

To do anything less is not only a detriment to your productivity, happiness, and all the other good things you are doing; it also robs you, your family, and your best customers of the positive attention they deserve.

So, stop yelling at your cat! Let it go. And move on.

CHAPTER THIRTEEN: THE BIG TAKE-AWAY

It's easy to get caught up stressing about things that our beyond our control. However, indulging in this type of behavior is completely counter-productive. Save yourself the trouble of expending your energy where it does not serve, and make an effort to focus only on the aspects of your business that you can influence for the better.

CHAPTER FOURTEEN
THE BIG LESSON: BEING AN EXPERT ISN'T ENOUGH

*"Nothing is more humiliating than to see idiots
succeed in enterprises we have failed in."*
—*Gustave Flaubert*

We all have a crazy story about how we ended up where we are, in this interesting niche profession of content marketing.

When I first broke out on my own and created my business, I thought of myself as a solid expert in my field. I had more than 20 years of experience in content and product development and felt like I had *earned* my right to succeed in my new endeavors.

However, when I didn't make money or have much success at first, I got sort of angry... and even a bit self-righteous. I felt that I simply "should" be able to pay myself more for the extensive hours I was putting into the business, especially considering all of the years of experience and dedication I had put into my field.

It was a defeating feeling.

Plus, as if adding insult to the injury, it seemed that other thought leaders in my field, even those who had half as much or even much less experience than myself *were* somehow making money.

I didn't get it.

Secretly, I would think to myself, "How are all of these bozos getting paid?"

One day, I finally asked my good friend, Mike Koenigs (who is not a bozo, rather he is one of my most respected friends, as well as an extremely savvy online marketer) for help.

"Mike," I said, "Why are you making money, and I'm not?"

His response was pretty simple (at least in retrospect). "Being an expert and having an idea is not the same as executing that idea. The value of idea is your *execution*, which in this case is your ability to effectively market that idea," he said.

I finally got it.

I had been so caught up in being an "expert" that I had overlooked what was lacking in me as an entrepreneur.

An entrepreneur is a person who organizes and operates a business. And in the field of content marketing, development, and delivery, it is someone who knows how to *use* information to drive sales.

Furthermore, great businesses create repeatable and consistent systems to sell goods and services that continually bring in revenue without the business owner having to be there *all the time*.

Whereas an expert's role is find ways to create engagement-worthy content, an entrepreneur's role is to find ways to create and build *processes that make money*.

I know a lot of broke experts—and I was one of them when I first started out. However, I also know a lot of successful entrepreneurs… who are experts "on the side."

You don't get paid by the hour to be an entrepreneur. And you don't get paid based on past your experience, or knowledge, or connections either. In fact, the number of hours you put into your field to qualify as an expert has absolutely no correlation with how much money you will make as a business owner... and you absolutely cannot take this personally.

As an entrepreneur, you will get paid *if and only if* you are able to set up a commerce cycle that works.

This takes practice. It requires a shift in focus from working to become a better expert, to getting better at business. Your message has to lead to money, or you won't be able to sustain your own self-employment.

Your greatest goal is not necessarily to get better at creating content, it is to improve your selling skills, your influencing skills, and your marketing skills, because these are the types of activities that will help you increase your paycheck. (Reading this book is a great step in the right direction!)

And although it may take some extra time up front to figure out a solid business plan that really works for you, the payoff down the road is a sustainable income. Once you establish processes that work, the business will no longer rely solely on you to function.

As a result, you will be free to continue to look for new ways to grow and improve your enterprise... which you will continually want to do—the minute you stop changing and growing, you start dying.

So keep challenging yourself. Keep looking for creative new ways to improve your business systems and to market your ideas.

As Confucius once said,

"By three methods we may learn wisdom. First, by reflection, which is the noblest; second by imitation, which is the easiest; and third by experience, which is the bitterest..."

But the best.

CHAPTER FOURTEEN: THE BIG TAKE-AWAY

By shifting your focus from who you are as an expert to who you are as an entrepreneur, you will be able to think about your business from a new vantage point—one that will encourage you to improve in areas that can directly improve your bottom line, as well as the longevity of your business.

"

The first sign of greatness is when a man does not attempt to look and act great.

—*Dale Carnegie*

FINAL THOUGHTS

"Because he believes in himself,
he doesn't try to convince others.
Because he is content with himself,
he doesn't need others' approval.
Because he accepts himself,
the whole world accepts him."
—*Tao Te Ching*

My goal in writing this book was to put a simple structure in place to help you create, distribute, and put what you know to work for you.

However, I hope that you have taken away much more from this book than just about "content marketing" or "content creation."

I hope that you feel ready to create your own personal content strategy. I hope you feel equipped to expand your reach, build your brand, close more sales, and... transform more lives.

I hope that instead of working so hard and constantly trying to *do* so much that you are motivated to be more precise, and therefore, effective in your content marketing efforts.

I hope that you are already looking for more ways to make your message relevant.

I hope that you will start to see yourself as an always-evolving entrepreneur versus simply as a content expert.

And mostly, I hope that you will be inspired to build the kind of relationships with your clients that really matter.

This year marks the 7th anniversary of the celebration of my mom's life.

And no matter how much time passes, I can still remember that day as vividly as if it were yesterday.

Right before the services started, a woman whom I did not recognize approached me. As she drew nearer, she explained that she had been one of my mom's original piano students.

She then went on to tell me that during college she had gone through a really rough period, and had even attempted suicide. But that during that time, the *only* person whose advice she trusted and who was able to give her the perspective and support she needed to move forward in life, was my mom.

I was blown away.

This woman had actually flown all the way from Dallas to be at the ceremony in upstate New York. And when I met her, it was obvious that she is now leading a beautiful life. She even showed me pictures of husband and her son, and told me that she was certain she wouldn't even be here today had it not been for the impact my mom had on her.

Then as we wrapped up our conversation, music began to fill the church.

And for possibly the hundredth time that day, I was moved to tears… because the sound coming from the chapel was incredible. Jonathan Boyd, a well-known opera singer, had just started to sing an impeccable version of *Brother James Air.*

He had called me a few days earlier, as we were preparing for the ceremony.

"Hey Pam, this is Jonathan Boyd. Your mom was my piano teacher, and I made a promise to her 30 years ago that I'd sing this song, *Brother James Air*, at her service, and I intend to keep that promise. I fly in Friday—when can I rehearse with the choir?"

The last time I remember seeing Jonathan, he had been struggling in school. He was in the principal's office every other week, had failed English, and and the general consensus was that he was going to struggle to even make it through high school.

I remember when he would come over for his piano lesson with my mom—they would usually play the piano for about five minutes, and then just go outside to bike around the block a few times.

30 years later, and… Jonathan is now a world-renowned opera singer. Wow.

Somehow, even when no one else could, my mom was able to see the best in him. She always knew what he was capable of and believed that all she had to do was help him find that special gift within himself.

And at least partly because of her support and encouragement, Jonathan is now traveling the world with his wife, singing operas in French, German, and Italian. This kid who no one thought would be able to make it through high school English, much less high school, is now speaking (and singing) several different languages, while living the life of his dreams.

And by keeping this promise and honoring my mom in this way, I was touched beyond words.

Oftentimes, we don't even realize the impact we have on others until much further down the road. In fact, we may not ever really know the difference we've made.

And although my mom didn't get to see the profound impact she had had on all her students so many years ago, it was extremely moving for me to connect with all of the people who honored her influence in their lives.

In fact, seeing these amazing people come together to celebrate my mom's influence on their lives changed my life perspective. It reminded me why I love sharing my knowledge and experiences to help others.

Like my mom, I believe in people.

I believe in you.

I believe that you have something worth sharing with the world.

I believe that it's important for you to do so.

And *that* is what this book is really about. It is about *you* getting *your unique knowledge, expertise, and perspective* out there to help the human beings around you create excellence in their lives.

I believe this will make the world a better place.

And I believe that *you* have the power to make this sort *impact* in the lives of others.

Starting now.

Be sure to access these implementation tools as my gift to you:

33 Ways to Use Content to Attract Leads and Build Your Business guide to give you ideas, strategies and tools you can use right now to start building your audience and your revenue.

Content Marketing Resource Guide with my favorite go-to solutions to save you TONS of time.

www.PamHendrickson.com/Impact

 3830 Valley Centre Drive #705-314, San Diego, CA 92130
866.654.6534 • 858.720.8720

Made in the USA
San Bernardino, CA
11 June 2016